ROBIN LANE FOX

Thoughtful Gardening

Great Plants, Great Gardens,
Great Gardeners

PENGUIN BOOKS

PENGUIN BOOKS

Published by the Penguin Group
Penguin Books Ltd, 80 Strand, London WC2R ORL, England
Penguin Group (USA) Inc., 375 Hudson Street, New York, New York 10014, USA
Penguin Group (Canada), 90 Eglinton Avenue East, Suite 700, Toronto, Ontario, Canada M4P 2Y3
(a division of Pearson Penguin Canada Inc.)
Penguin Ireland, 25 St Stephen's Green, Dublin 2, Ireland (a division of Penguin Books Ltd)
Penguin Group (Australia), 707 Collins Street, Melbourne, Victoria 3008, Australia
(a division of Pearson Australia Group Pty Ltd)
Penguin Books India Pvt Ltd, 11 Community Centre, Panchsheel Park, New Delhi – 110 017, India
Penguin Group (NZ), 67 Apollo Drive, Rosedale, Auckland 0632, New Zealand
(a division of Pearson New Zealand Ltd)
Penguin Books (South Africa) (Pty) Ltd, Block D, Rosebank Office Park,
181 Jan Smuts Avenue, Parktown North, Gauteng 2193, South Africa

Penguin Books Ltd, Registered Offices: 80 Strand, London WC2R ORL, England

www.penguin.com

First published by Particular Books 2010
Published in Penguin Books 2013
001

Copyright © Robin Lane Fox, 2010

Set in 9.25/12.5pt Sabon LT Std
Typeset by Jouve (UK), Milton Keynes
Printed in England by Clays Ltd, St Ives plc

ISBN: 978-0-141-04594-8

www.greenpenguin.co.uk

ALWAYS LEARNING   **PEARSON**

The practising gardener is always a Martha; it is Mary who sits back in admiration, saying how pretty that looks! Mary thinks it has just happened, as a gift from heaven; Mary is a dreamer, overlooking the practical pains and trouble that have gone to the making of the effect Mary admires. Mary can just sit. Martha, if she can spare the time for it, can and must sit and think.

Vita Sackville-West, in The Observer,
6 October 1957

Contents

CONTENTS

Summer

Autumn

List of Illustrations

Preface

Most people begin to garden only when they have a garden of their own, and some people begin only when their most important seedlings, their own children, have grown up. A few of us began gardening much earlier, in our own parents' space and time. I began when I was ten years old and by the age of twelve was a seriously keen grower of alpine plants. I have continued ever since, widening the range of plants which I have known, grown and killed personally. I cannot fully express what gardening has added to my life, ever-present in my mind and increasingly in my muscles, and always adding more to what I notice in the daily course of living. It has also brought many remarkable people to me, a few of whom this book honours. It has deepened what I find in books and poems and in great paintings, the identity of whose flowers is so seldom considered by their curators and historians.

This book aims to look at gardening from many different aspects, swiftly changing as if under a kaleidoscope. So much more could have been included, but I like the variety and balance in what it contains. I believe I have grown all the plants which it mentions if they are plants which grow outdoors on alkaline soil. When I left school I worked for some months in the great Botanical Garden in Munich where I was assigned to the fine Alpinum with its geographically arranged mountain flora and its acres of imported rock, brought in by railway in the first decade of the twentieth century. I have never forgotten the lessons I learned or the human dramas of those days, but I am less willing nowadays to begin work before 7 a.m. and I no longer line up with seventy-seven others to be ticked off on lists kept by the garden's

Gruppenführer in a pleasantly earthy seed room. I regret the loss of the edelweiss braces that held up my trousers, but this book recalls subsequent lessons, many of them learned in great English gardens where I have lived or been a frequent visitor. Above all it is based on my good fortune in being responsible for two very different types of garden, the big garden round my Oxford college and the two-acre garden round my house on poor stony soil in the Cotswolds.

Many of my chapters have grown and evolved from articles first written for the *Financial Times*, for which I have been a weekly columnist on gardening for no less than forty uninterrupted years. In January 1970 I was offered a trial column by the paper's legendary editor, Gordon Newton, in the belief that the *FT* needed brightening up on Wednesdays. I even survived my initial observation that the flowers on the great man's desk were plastic, but I did not expect him to become an ever keener gardener, growing excellent fuchsias and much else in his years of retirement. I sometimes wonder where the impetus to write, usually so happily, comes from each week. I trace its roots to my Eton days at boarding school where I used to read E. B. Anderson's superb book on rock gardening by torchlight under the bedclothes, and where my request for special leave to visit the Chelsea Flower Show was known to be genuine and was duly granted, but only with a female chaperone, my tutor's wife, in case I cut loose among the rival attractions of London. I would not even have known how to find them. In Windsor's nearby public library I then tracked down the books of gardening articles by Vita Sackville-West, written for *The Observer* between 1946 and 1961. They remain the best gardening articles which I and so many others have read, and I never imagined that one day I would be asked to re-read her work in full and present another selection of it. After discovering these short masterpieces, which she herself professed to disdain, I became joint editor of the school newspaper, the 'Eton Chronicle', and even then, the writing of casual columns and editorials struck me as something I could do and whose deadlines I enjoyed.

Years of undergraduate terms in Oxford then followed in which active gardening was impossible, although I made up for some of the loss by enjoying the setting of my then college's Addison's Walk, at that time the most beautiful tamed landscape in England. Early Christian desert fathers sometimes hint at the pull of the desert in their ascetic decision to abandon the settled world. Addison's Walk and its meadow's glory, its wild fritillaries, exerted some of the pull behind my realization that I, too, would never wholly live in everyday society. At that time I was writing essays twice weekly for my tutors and I thought that as I could do two, it would be easy to write only one, this time on the gardening I loved. I never imagined that I would write more than two thousand consecutively.

I owed my crucial editorial interview to the interest of Pat Gibson and also to the instincts of Lord Drogheda, such important figures in the *FT* company's life and examples of how to encourage young aspirants to see if they can really perform. I have since owed much to the apt laissez-faire approach of successive editors, especially Geoffrey Owen, Richard Lambert, and nowadays Lionel Barber. For years I contributed in handwriting or by telephone and I thank especially Mary Dorwald and the varied teams of *FT* copytakers, headed by the imperturbable Mandy with whom I, like many others, had the ideal telephone relationship before she emigrated, without ever meeting me in person, while her supporting staff withdrew to new lives in bars across the Mediterranean.

My gardening is done in time stolen from other work, as it is also done in the lives of so many *FT* readers. I owe special debts to helpers and encouragers in the garden, especially my parents and our beloved gardener Leslie Aris in distant years which seem like yesterdays, and those who help me regularly nowadays, Marius Hardiman and Jim Marriott and their respective teams in Oxford, and Marcia Little and Terry Wheeler at my home. Not all the great moments in gardening are solitary and I and my present garden owe much to our duet with Caroline Badger at a crucial time.

As for this book, Stuart Proffitt made me write it, a far more demanding task than I anticipated. Many people in recent years have told me to do it and one or two have tried to buy it in bookshops before it was even commissioned. I am immensely grateful to Tatjana Mitevska for her skilled work in retrieving long-lost bits of text and her ebullient support in so many ways. Neil O'Sullivan deserves special thanks for his intelligent editing over the years and his patience with my anxious transition to a digital future. Nicholas Spencer and Raphael Abraham are worthy successors in the weekly turmoil of *FT* life. My pupils Robert Colborn and Henry Mason skilfully decoded and typed my text, while retaining an amused incredulity at subjects so far removed from their own. Jane Birdsell was the most penetrating questioner as copy-editor and practising gardener and has saved me from several errors. I am particularly grateful for the kind guidance of the many libraries, photographers, nurseries, and Dr Jane Lightfoot who helped me with the business of finding or taking relevant pictures. Dr Claudia Wagner rose to the challenge of tracing so much, so far removed from her expertise in classical art and engraved gems.

I remember my remarkable grandmother Enid wondering why I wanted to go to Oxford and fearing, wisely, that I 'might become a don or something frightful'. Gardening, on the other hand, always seemed to her to be worth encouraging and so, in her wake, I continue to think that I have compensated for the one by combining it with the other.

Thoughtful Gardening

Gardening is a thoughtful activity, but thinkers tend to look down on it. It is practical and repetitive, they think, and it is often very dirty. A few universities give degrees in landscape design and professional horticulture, but their emphasis is on weed-suppression and mass propagation. They do not give degrees in practical gardening and its relation to art and science. I have heard thinkers blame the English love of gardening for England's industrial failure. I have even heard them dismiss gardening as a substitute for proper study, a reason, they think, why women are so keen on it, as many of them, now middle-aged, supposedly never had a proper education 'instead'. When I began gardening, more than fifty years ago, the distinguished Professor of Medicine in Oxford was telling the young male doctors in his department that there were two important rules in life. They must live within walking distance of the hospital and they must not buy a house with a garden too big for their wife to manage.

There are exceptions, including exceptional thinkers. Before I came to Oxford at the age of eighteen I had worked for months in the great alpine garden of the Botanical Garden in Munich, one on a staff of seventy-eight. In my second year of Oxford study, I moved on to philosophy and found a hero in a world of thought which otherwise seemed far beyond my grasp. The famous thinker Ludwig Wittgenstein had the attraction of being described to me by my judicious tutor as 'decidedly rum'. So I tracked down a lecture which the 'rum' Wittgenstein had given in Cambridge in 1929 and marvelled to find him remarking that sometimes he 'wondered at the existence of the world' and at others, that he knew the 'experience of feeling absolutely safe'.

He sounded so neurotic to my earth-bound mind. It seemed interestingly odd that he thought, 'How extraordinary that anything should exist.' It seemed even odder that he thought, 'I am safe, nothing can injure me whatever happens,' and believed that others thought so too. It was hard to believe that he had lived among brothers and sisters, let alone that he was the youngest of eight. Clearly he had not lived my daily life with horses, and surely he had never weeded among nettles.

I then found that he had fought in the First World War, a fact which helped to explain his interest in 'feeling absolutely safe'. I also found that he had thought about 'thoughtful activity'. 'Let us imagine,' he had written, 'someone doing work that involves comparison, trial, choice', constructing something out of 'various bits of stuff with a given set of tools. Every now and then, there is the problem, "Should I use *this* bit?" The bit is rejected, another is tried . . .' Wittgenstein was imagining the 'construction of an appliance', but he could as well have been describing my work in Munich's alpine garden, where I dug with a pointed German version of a straight-edged English spade and planted lemon-flowered trollius among blue Bavarian gentians in the belief that they would go well together in acid soil. Wittgenstein went on to imagine the 'whole procedure' being filmed. 'The worker perhaps also produces sound-offerings like "hm" or "ha!"': in my German garden, Herr Strauss would burp and Herr Schmidt notoriously farted. Neither in Munich nor in Wittgenstein's notebook did the worker 'utter a single word'. He was thinking, nonetheless: 'of course we cannot separate his "thinking" from his activity. For, the thinking is not an accompaniment of the work, any more than of thoughtful speech.' During my first year in Oxford I had been convinced that I had thought more while gardening in Munich than I had yet been made to think by a tutor in classical Greek. Now, this great thinker, so 'rum' to my teacher, was endorsing my belief. Thoughtful gardening became my creed.

There was still a gap between the philosopher's idea of it and mine. His worker worked thoughtfully, but he did not think long and hard before he started, and he did not put his thoughts into words. His thinking was rudimentary, but when I read on, I learned more. Wittgenstein, I found, had twice worked as a gardener for several months in his life. My hero became a demi-god and though I understood so little, I read whatever I could find of his writings. In summer 1920, I discovered, he had been training to teach in a primary school in Austria, but he had spent the vacation working in the gardens round the monastery at Klosterneuburg, close to Vienna and even closer to the River Danube. While he gardened, no doubt thoughtfully, the abbot of the monastery passed by the flowerbed and remarked, 'So, I see that intelligence counts for something in gardening too.'

It is a pity that the abbot cannot read this book. For thirty years I have had the honour of running the gardens at my Oxford college, New College, in a world of thinkers for whom I also run nine outlying gardens, including some in which they think, but do not work. I oversee the valiant teams of contractors who work for us three days a week from March until December, and I discuss the lawns with the man who cuts them when sent on secondment from the College's grassy sports grounds. Like Wittgenstein's thoughtful worker, I choose, I compare, I try, and perhaps I 'hm' and 'ha!'. Nothing is planted or changed without my orders. The gardeners do the work, but I supplement them at weekends or on evenings when the season is at its most challenging and my own Cotswold garden allows me to be unfaithful. Around me, undergraduates go about their thinking business, without time to wonder that the world exists or the audacity to feel entirely safe. My colleagues, some of them fellow tutors, are paid to think daily too, but I seldom know what they think about the garden beyond an unwondering sense that it exists. Some of them have the oddest ideas about gardening. Our academic year begins in October, and on one such beginning a colleague invited me to drinks in order to celebrate the new year. One thinking guest had just returned from a summer spent testing rats in a foreign laboratory and put a question to me which brought me up with a bump. 'Have you had a good summer too, Robin? Were the flowers all the right colours?'

If gardening has something to do with intelligence, my colleagues sometimes make me wonder where the intelligence lies. The thoughtful gardeners in this book are not people with acclaimed intellectual minds. They include Lady Chatterley's lover and the head gardener of a great house in Northamptonshire near the poet John Clare. For more than forty years my College gardens employed another one, a former prisoner-of-war from Poland who had chosen to live on in England when the world war ended. He worked on the land and ended up weeding in our College grounds. His greying hair grew ever longer, his teeth were reduced to a necessary few, and the upper half of his gumboots remained folded down in all weathers. In the winter months he worked steadily to build a garden cart from wooden planks and when at last it was finished, his fellow gardeners towed him on a lap of honour round the garden paths. He stood proudly in the centre of the cart, holding his garden scythe in a pose which Italian artists ascribe to Death, the grim reaper, in their paintings of his triumphal procession.

The time came for him to retire to the wooden house up a ladder which he had built on a patch of Oxford's allotments and owned after many years of unchallenged occupation. I proposed the usual retirement party, to the scepticism of those who had to organize it, but on the day appointed, the honorand was present, dressed in an unexpectedly smart suit of pin-striped grey. A small group of colleagues waited for the head of the College to attend and make the presentation. We waited, and eventually our head appeared, only to sit down at the piano in the room and give us a stilted version of a piano rag by Scott Joplin. Breaking off, he beamed at the audience over his bow tie and asked, soliciting approval, 'I love boogie-woogie: don't you love boogie-woogie too?' From the back row, the voice of our retiring gardener broke the silence, then silenced us all: 'Personally, I prefer Donizetti.'

Meanwhile, in sunny weather, the thinking undergraduates roll and kiss on the lawns and try to read books with titles like *The Constant Flux*. They are respectful to the plants and are aware of change in the borders without thinking that gardening is only a search for flowers of the right colour. However, as their final year comes to an end they show signs of having caught their thinking tutors' prejudices. They tell me that they do hope I will be around to meet their parents, because their mothers would so much like advice on gardening. When I meet them, what the mothers want is an appreciation of their sons and daughters.

The undergraduates leave, but there is an alarming hole in their knowledge of the world. In more than thirty-five years of teaching them, I have asked from time to time if one of them knows what a primrose looks like. They may have read poetry by Milton or Herrick, and they may even have scored a distinction in plant sciences. Not one of them has ever known a primrose. Recently, there was a moment of hope with a boy from Ireland who told me that of course he knew, it was a pretty flower and it appeared in spring. Expectation soared, but he then went on to say that it was 'sort of rounded and purple, like a cup' which he outlined with his big hands.

I should have given up the question but I tried it one more time on a sharp-eyed young lady, who perhaps evoked it by her choice of scent. In early March, while she read me her essay on changes in classical Spartan society, a cheap scent of bluebells floated on the air. As we ended our hour of teaching, I asked her about her holiday plans, her choice of subjects for next term and, fatally incited by the bluebells, whether she knew what a primrose looked like. She squirmed disdainfully into the sofa and fixed me with a look which had a future in high finance stamped over it. 'That's a really pedantic question,' she replied, 'I see exactly the same flowers as you do, but you just put academic names on them.'

I left for lunch, feeling battered by this young nihilist who had reduced me to a 'superfluous person', like nature-loving father Nikolay in Turgenev's *Fathers and Sons*. I sat myself next to Oxford's Professor of Logic and I retold this exchange, conveying my belief that naming deepens knowledge and encourages closer distinctions in what we see. Philosophical depths threatened to open and the professor fell silent, pushed the last of his food round his plate and looked so uneasy that I thought I had trampled on a logical rule. Eventually he volunteered that he had something to tell me: 'I do not know what a primrose looks like, either.'

Two weeks later I caught him by the sleeve of his pale-fawn mackintosh and took him out into the garden where the grass was alive with primroses and blue anemones beamed under a sunny sky. I even picked a primrose and gave it to him, to which he remarked, 'So, that is it.' Wittgenstein could not have put it more concisely. His ladyfriend then told me that he had put the flower in water and kept it on his desk. There was hope, I thought, but two days later I had a card of thanks and a copy of a famous philosophical article on Meaning and Reference. One of its author's points was that a word seems to have a different sort of scope if it is used by speakers who have differing degrees of knowledge about its reference. The author tried to clarify his argument with an example. 'Suppose you are like me and cannot tell an elm from a beech tree . . .' I was fighting an uphill battle. I can show logicians a primrose, but I can no longer show them an elm tree. Except for a small group in Sussex, mature elms have been killed by beetles.

I returned to reading Wittgenstein, hoping that his months behind a wheelbarrow would have left a deeper mark on his thinking. In his *Brown Book*, I duly found him reflecting on some bedding-out. 'A friend and I,' he wrote, 'once looked at beds of pansies. Each bed showed a different kind. We were impressed by each in turn. Speaking about them, my friend said, "What a variety of colour patterns and each says something." And this was just what I myself wished to say.' It was not at all what I would have wished to say myself. 'How pretty,' or 'How ugly,' I might have said, or 'What a Germanic style of planting.' Disappointingly, Wittgenstein had had no such thoughts. 'If one had asked,' he went on, 'what the colour pattern of the pansy said, the right answer would have seemed to be that it said itself.' The obvious answer seemed to me that pansy-patterns 'say' nothing at all.

I have not called this book 'Talking to Pansies', and even from Wittgenstein's example, I conclude that thoughtful gardening has yet to dig itself in deeply among thinkers all around me. My text and title aim to promote it and answer that young serpent on my sofa. Thinking and knowing do not lead to pedantic labelling from an over-academic mind: they enhance what we see. Thoughtful gardeners think before choosing and planting, so I will share the thoughts on specific plants and their preferences which my own experiments have confirmed. Sometimes I will pass on lessons which expert growers have taught me, because I believe that those who depend on growing plants for their livelihood are most likely to know how to do it, although they are usually too busy to write their knowledge down.

Sometimes I have learned through travel, which makes me think less parochially, so I describe my thoughts about gardens which lie far beyond my own. I hope that these gardens will be helpful magnets for gardeners who are fellow travellers too. Above all I have learned from fellow writers and practitioners, to some of whom I pay a posthumous tribute for the impact of their life's work on what I think and do.

The thoughtful gardening of this book is flower gardening, and though practically based, it is linked at times to fiction or poetry. They are not distractions, because they, too, help gardeners to see more. This way of evocative viewing goes back to Chinese scholar-gardeners whose reading and poetry shaped their gardens' names and designs. In the West it began much later with Erasmus, who described and regarded a sixteenth-century garden through associations which the plants acquired from his reading. Erasmus was not a working gardener himself, but reading deepened what a garden meant to him, as it still deepens what mine means to me.

Above all, thoughtful gardening helps gardeners to realize what flower gardening is about. It has become confused with so many other aims, 'saving the planet', 'working for biodiversity', 'reviving a lost world' or 'creating a matrix of linked habitats'. It is none of those things. It means trying to grow plants well, whatever their origins, and placing them in a setting which suits them and us. In pursuit of this aim, it is not wrong to use chemicals and it is impractical and ineffective to use only 'organic' methods. There is no 'organic' killer for bindweed or lily beetles. Nor is it wrong to prefer short-lived, exotic flowers or to love dahlias and chrysanthemums in bright colours, although 'natural' gardening is supposed to despise them. All gardeners cultivate an artificial landscape, even if their minds have modelled it on 'nature' or a 'wildflower meadow'. Artful pretence is rooted in all gardens, but thoughtful gardening practises its pretences in a conscious, independent way. It is not governed by bossy fashion. A classic herbaceous border is not more laborious than a fashionable sweep of rudbeckias and ornamental grasses which pretend to be a prairie. Gardens are not 'havens for wildlife', because 'wildlife' will scuffle in them and uproot the plants. Nor are gardeners 'restoring' a population of threatened butterflies. Gardeners' help to them is infini-tesimal in the total picture and is short-lived in the wider context of farming and climatic change with which butterflies must cope beyond the garden fence. Gardening is dulled and limited if defined by moral purposes which are driven by other concerns.

Thoughtful gardening leads instead to knowledge, an asset which is intertwined with gardening's roots. In the first legendary garden stood a tree of knowledge and when our parents ate its fruit, the woman first, the man second, thoughtful gardening was born. The garden, they realized, was no longer the entire world. Ejected from it, they found that plants do not always grow in divine profusion. Hence-forward they had to think while they dug and toiled and made 'comparison, trial and choice'. They thought above all of the garden they had lost, just as thoughtful gardeners still think of gardens they once knew. This thought, too, is explored in this book.

Winter

Prune Cobnuts and Filberts. Cobnuts and filberts must be pruned as soon as the small red flowers can be seen. These are rather insignificant and you must look closely to find them. It is the male catkins that make the show. The leading shoots of established bushes which fill their space are shortened to a couple of buds each. If there is still room for the bushes to extend there is no need to prune these leaders at all, or at the most only to remove their tips. Side shoots are cut back to the first catkin, reckoning from the tip, or, if there are no catkins, to the first female flower. Some shoots may have catkins only. These should be left unpruned until the catkins fade and then be cut right back to two buds. There is no point in keeping them, as they will not produce any nuts. Badly placed branches which crowd up the centre of the bush should be removed altogether, even if this means using a saw. The ideal nut bush is roughly in the form of a goblet.

Arthur Hellyer, 'February: Fourth Week', in his
Your Garden Week by Week *(1936; sixth edition, 1992)*

Winters respond to thoughtful gardening. They have their short, cold spells, which limit choices for gardens outside warmer cities, and there are also those days of dark rain and gale-warnings, some of which come true. Their boundaries, however, are advancing with the warmer average temperatures of the past twenty years and there are many more days of clear, surprising sunshine than traditional wet in a modern 'fill-dyke' February. Great gardeners have sometimes invited me to see their gardens in late winter, agreeing with Valerie Finnis (whom I honour in my Spring section) that the garden looks its best in February. I now see what they mean. Early camellias, the heavenly scent on upright *Daphne bholua* 'Jacqueline Postill', dozens of *Helleborus × hybridus* and as many crocuses as the local wildlife leaves un-excavated: these flowers stand out in the year's first sunshine against the bare tracery of trees, the white bark of a good birch tree (*Betula jacquemontii* being one of the best), and a firm evergreen framework of box, osmanthus and glistening pittosporum.

In late January, I have learned to induce the daffodil season prematurely by planting the excellent *Narcissus* 'Rijnveld's Early Sensation', otherwise marketed as 'January Gold'. It shows yellow trumpet-daffodils at a height of only a foot and persists for weeks even if a sharp frost causes the flowers to lie for a while on the ground. Often, 'January Gold' waits until early February in colder parts of Britain, but it is a superb variety and completely hardy. It is a magical anticipation of spring, rabbit-proof, badger-proof and very easily grown. It has an excellent twin, the pale-flowered 'Spring Dawn' which also has trumpet flowers at this manageable height, but combines light yellow and white most prettily. They are soon followed by the smaller *Narcissus* 'February Gold', another winner except that it flowers with me in March; and then by its bright attendants, 'Jack Snipe' and 'Tête-à-Tête', whose yellow flowers are held in small groupings. I use these smaller narcissi in animal-proof groups for the gaps of bare earth in summer's borders. They are essential accompaniments to the end of winter.

On intervening days, there is time to recall, even to visit, gardens in summer settings abroad. I address this aspect of winter through my memories of the first garden in which I lived as an adult and its remarkable lady owner. I also evoke other thoughtful gardeners, active from Morocco to Texas and back to Great Dixter in Sussex. In winter there is time to travel, and I have learned so much about the range of shrubs which will flower from January to March by travelling to the fine Hillier Gardens near Ampfield in Hampshire, developed by the expert Harold Hillier and maintained so impressively by Hampshire County Council after his death. As I live on alkaline soil, I have dwelt here on shrubs which will tolerate lime, among which I would emphasize the early flowering varieties of *Viburnum × bodnantense*, 'Dawn' and 'Deben' being the best-known favourites and 'Charles Lamont' as good as them both. When taken indoors, their flowers have a peppery scent which is sweet but strong. They are essential in the backbone of all thoughtfully planted gardens. The superb witch hazels, or hamamelis, are essential too and well shown in the Hillier Gardens, but are denied to me by the limey soil which they dislike. In the first half of the year gardeners on acid soil have a wider range of choice.

Between reading, reflecting and relishing the early narcissi, I choose the year's half-hardy annuals, usually by sending away for seeds because the seed-racks in garden centres can only display a restricted range. Some of these seeds need to be sown promptly in a heated greenhouse, especially the tall white-flowered *Nicotiana sylvestris*, the tobacco plant which does not catch powdery mildew but which needs an early start and plenty of water throughout the year if it is to develop its big leaves and retain a fresh green. The plants should be potted on into individual four-inch pots before they finally go outdoors, protected by slug bait, in late May. With them, I sow seeds of gazanias, so good in pots and the corners of flowerbeds, especially in the bold 'Tiger Stripe' variety whose yellow-orange flowers are lined with brown. Gazanias profit from an early start because they too can be grown on individually in pots and planted out earlier in May, when they will survive a slight frost. They need direct sunlight for their flowers to open fully.

In mid- to late February I sow the excellent *Antirrhinum* 'Royal Bride' from Thompson & Morgan, a tall variety with long spikes of scented white flowers which repeat well after dead-heading. It out-lasts all the others which I have tried in the family. I also start off the mainstays of my bedding-out: tall white-flowered cosmos daisies. The most widely available seed packets contain *Cosmos bipinnatus* 'Sonata', a shorter and duller variety, whereas 'Purity' is taller and bigger-flowered, and the tallest of all is 'Cosmonaut', with semi-double flowers. They too can be potted individually and stopped by pinching out their main stem in order to encourage side-branches and yet more flowers. They respond best to regular watering when first planted out and to constant dead-heading when they flower, a trick which prolongs them until October's frost. At the same time I sow the invaluable rudbeckias, so reliable in any summer. The toughest pretty mixture is still 'Rustic Dwarf', but the best individual flowers come from the recent hybrid 'Prairie Sun', an outstandingly good variety with flat flowers of a sunny yellow and a stamina which keeps it in flower, two feet high, until late October. Rudbeckias are my answer to the unpredictability of modern summers, because they flourish in sea-sons wet or dry. In late March, lastly, my zinnia seeds go in, because the seedlings grow so quickly and dislike being checked for a while before going out in late May, and so they are best moved only once, directly into individual pots. Zinnias are prettiest in traditional big-flowered mixtures with scarlet and yellow shades. If they are muted or reduced in height and flower-size, they lose their special charm.

None of these plants can be bought cheaply on the market in early summer. By mid-February, active gardening extends beyond the green-houses to the garden itself. It is accompanied by the first unwelcome patter of four-legged feet, which I describe here not because I dislike animals but because I do not want them in a delicate garden of flowers. Most of them are welcome to proliferate outside the garden's fence, but just as a weed is a plant in the wrong place, so a wild animal in a flower-garden is generally a pest. February causes such animal turbulence, driving elderly badgers into exile and male foxes far afield to find female mates. Gardeners need to be vigilant to survive the symptoms, while taking advantage of the fine-weather days for an early start. Time used early in the year is time freed during the spring rush. I try to weed and aerate the borders by early March, ready for mulches wherever I wish to apply layers of leaf-mould on the soil's surface. It is not an organic food. I prefer to use efficient artificial fertilizer, not inefficient natural compost, as the source of the important chemicals for a plant's roots. The value of a leafy top-dressing is that it opens and improves the structure of the soil, making the roots' life easier. Thickly applied, it will also help to keep in natural moisture, a reason why mulches are best applied after a wet winter or a wet spell in spring. 'Organic' is merely a seductive word, and it was first applied to nature, so far as I know, by D. H. Lawrence. His contribution to passionate gardening will feature in my Spring section, but his ideal of 'organicity' is not one which I share. Nor is it a universal imperative. Sometimes, flowerbeds are better left unmulched, without organic matter, especially if they are made of free-draining soil and planted with plants from stony, poor habitats. Not everything worth growing in nature grows best in the spongy, rotting compost which is pushed at modern gardeners. It is restrictive to be an 'organic' gardener only, and over time I have learned to be eclectic, using inorganic compounds on pests, weeds and plants which need extra chemicals, and organic materials only where the soil is too poor or too heavy for the plants which I want to grow in it. Both types of material, organic and inorganic, deliver similar chemicals to plants' roots. As 'feeds', they vary only in efficiency.

As in the garden, so indoors, there is profit in making an artful, early start. In the Spring section, I will refer to the willingness of ribes, or flowering currant, to flower early if it is cut when the first buds show on the stems and is brought into a warm room. In winter, even in mid-February, yellow-flowered forsythias will do likewise, opening some five or six weeks early and lighting up a house.

New Year Resolve

My new year is full of good intentions which it would be optimistic to call resolutions. In the garden, I will be more punctual. I will remember to feed everything in pots, even in the middle of their growing season. I will not leave flower bulbs unplanted in brown paper bags. I will try to stake in time, not on the morning after a collapse. I may even check for earwigs. I will not walk on the lawns during heavy frosts. I will remember to sow sweet william seeds for flowers in the following year and I will do the job in the first week of June. I will not throw stones at squirrels. Instead, I will buy a new squirrel-trap and bait it with peanut butter. When I catch one, I will take it in the car and let it out near the garden of the nearest member of parliament who voted to ban fox-hunting.

I will also address the needs of a garden which is in its middle age. It is amazing how things have not grown as I anticipated. The climbers on the walls are mostly too big. I never imagined that my avenues of upright hornbeams and *Pyrus calleryana* 'Chanticleer' would grow so tall and cost so much to cut and shape. I did not expect so many border plants to run wild on such a scale. At lower levels, some of the best small hardy plants have died of old age, a hazard which gardening books seldom mention. None of the dianthus even waited to become elderly, and I am bemused to realize how many I have replaced. I used to reckon that owners of raised beds in a garden had lost the plot when their beds became overrun with the bonfire-red flowers of zauschneria in autumn. Last autumn, my raised beds were a flaming zone of zauschnerias. My old mats of low-growing phloxes have brown patches in their middles. Ants have killed off a little erodium with red-eyed flowers, and something seems to have sat in the centre of my autumn-flowering gentians. I do not want to think about the superb small *Campanula* 'Lynchmere', which was at its best when I dug it up last year and tried to divide it. Its roots are the wrong shape for division and so it has died. I am not alone in finding it difficult to increase as it has now disappeared from many nurseries in the *Plant Finder*, the Royal Horticultural Society's guide to 'more than 70,000 plants and 640 places to buy them'.

The easiest way to treat middle-aged gardens is to leave them alone to become senile. The first sign of middle age is when owners talk about growing only the things which seem to suit them. Then those things get the upper hand and owners start to reclassify the planting as the 'meadow look'. That 'look' involves too many hardy geraniums and valerians and too many seedlings from the previous year's forget-me-nots. If I do not control *Rudbeckia fulgida* 'Goldsturm' this year, I will have to pretend that its border was planned years ago as a prairie. I also have to face the fact that so many of my worst invaders are plants for which I paid good money and which I introduced. Never accept an unnamed autumn-flowering helianthus. The family includes the rampant Jerusalem artichoke whose tubers are so hard to eradicate. Never plant white-flowered *Achillea ptarmica* 'The Pearl' or 'Perry's White' in a bed which is meant to be civilized. They are fine as cut flowers but their running white roots elude removal with a spade.

Here, resolve becomes relevant. Beginners and owners of new gardens start out with all their mistakes before them, whereas middle-aged gardeners live with mistakes already self-inflicted. Try to look at your ageing creations with the eye of an incoming owner. After one such look I commissioned some ruthless cutting and felling. Out went the dull, dusty sycamores and a middle-aged walnut tree which I inherited too near to the house. Half of my trees should have come out years ago, but I forget how I had to make my garden by demolishing a feathery forest. I uprooted more than a hundred tall leylandii cypresses with the help of a mechanical digger's front bucket when I took over the land and had to reopen its lawns and views. It is never too late in life to let in the light.

It is a myth that gardens will age gracefully and become peacefully mature over time. Gardens never stand still and never allow us to buy a season ticket on the line of least resistance. They need as much guiding, reshaping and rethinking in their twenty-fifth year as in their third. The past ten years of gardening on television and in beautifully illustrated magazines have lured many people into trying it as if it is exterior decoration which will be as obedient as a new lamp or sofa cover. When some plants die and others grow out of shape, they learn that the fun of real gardening is that it is never pinned down.

It will never pin me down. I have learned to trust my capacity for experiments which are at least two steps ahead of reality. I am someone who presented his garden with a laborious new swimming pool and promptly lost interest in swimming. For years Mother Nature has had the pool to herself and has turned it into a dramatic wilderness of self-sown buddleias and bullrushes. They are being sustained on a diet of the naturally drowned hedgehogs which float upwards in the winter months. For years I have been hoping that the water may spontaneously generate human life. Better still, it may prove the Bible right and present me with a female helpmate, a muscular clone of Eve. At least she will not need a work permit.

So far, the pool has produced only a batch of newts. My latest resolution is to restore its former shallow end to clear, rush-free water and plant it with white-flowering water lilies, contained in old car tyres. You know what resolutions are, but I like the idea of becoming that Japanese item, an 'artist of the floating world'. No doubt the lilies will turn out to be the next invaders of my own making.

'Tresco on Teesside'

How seriously should gardeners be planning for climate change? It is not an idle question for inactive days in the wake of a New Year lunch. Money is now being thrown at it and the fear of hot weather risks multiplying hot air of a different kind. The Royal Horticultural Society has jumped on a problem which it defines as 'Gardening in the Global Greenhouse'. The National Trust has held conferences on the way forward for the next eighty years. There is a UK Climate Impact Programme and the beginnings of a flood of literature to tell us what to do.

According to the RHS, English gardens can expect to see more loquats, pomegranates, Guadeloupe palm trees and a low-growing North African convolvulus which they have decided to call 'blue rock bindweed'. For hedges, 'good garden management', they urge, will choose oleanders, those dreaded shrubs which flourish round Italian petrol stations. Our gardens, they recommend, should include myrtles and trees of the albizia, which I have seen at its best in Delhi. Do they really believe these recommendations? Have they ever tried to garden in the orbit of Chipping Norton, let alone in unforgiving Derbyshire? Their summary report by two professors produced the airy generalization that 'Tresco has spread to Tunbridge Wells and is on its way to Teesside'. If so, its slipstream is passing many gardeners by. Only recently, we had eleven days of frost in the Cotswolds which killed several of my climbing roses, annihilated the evergreen ceanothus and wiped out established plants of what is considered to be a tough cistus, aptly named 'Snow White'.

In February 2009 and January 2010 we awoke to a deep and

beautiful 'winter wonderland' around the dreaming spires of Oxford. It killed off penstemons and destroyed the parahebes. If the National Trust is already discussing the 'impact', not the reality, of climate change, presumably its experts believe that the climate has changed to a new plateau. If they believe in this new plateau, it is only because they are judging it by statistical averages. They are ceasing to allow for the lethal capacity of continuing short, sharp snaps in the wider pattern. Mother Nature is inconsistent and I refuse to trust her, even when she dangles herself in a winter bikini.

We have no idea what the impact of possible global warming will be on Britain over the next eighty years. Some of the most respected experts warn us that one local effect may be bouts of intensified cold. All we know is that for the past fifteen years there has been less frost in most winters, a few very wet winters, more very dry ones and some turbulent storms. What does this variety mean? Whenever gardeners start talking about 'climatic shift', I turn back to an invaluably observed source, 'The Garden Calendar', maintained by the meticulous naturalist Gilbert White from 1751 to 1773 in Hampshire. Between 1757 and 1760 the winters were as mild as ours in the new millennium. On 26 December 1757, 'very mild weather: hardly any frost yet'. In 1758, it 'continued very mild, one short frost excepted, to the end of the year'. In 1759, on 19 January, he recorded that 'many kinds of flowers are got above ground some weeks before their usual times: the snowdrops and some crocuses were in bloom before old December was out'. On 18 December 1760, it was 'very mild growing weather yet: the grass in pastures has kept springing the whole season' and 'soft sunny days like April which brought the flies and other insects out of their lurking-places'. On 1 January 1761, he transplanted a multiheaded narcissus in full flower and brought it indoors. There was no National Trust to tell him to plant banana trees, which was fortunate because there were eleven days of continuous frost in December 1762 and on 31 December 1766 it 'froze under people's beds'. The weather swung between unusual mildness and sudden months or days of frost, just as ours still does. My firm advice to gardeners in the 2010s is therefore simple: do nothing. I refuse to believe that the Texas Palmetto and tender hedges of acacia can be expected to flourish in

English gardens in the next forty years. It takes only one night of old-fashioned behaviour by the British ice-demons to wipe them all out.

As always, scares can be multiplied, especially if there are gardening practices which, deep down, the scarers dislike. The National Trust and the RHS have even sent me warning documents about the spread of new insects and pests 'due to warmer average temperatures'. I am sceptical whether the zigzag pattern on our weather chart is the culprit. Bushes of berberis, they tell us, are now at risk of attack by a new type of sawfly which originates in southern Europe. Camellias are at risk from a new Japanese petal blight. The fundamental reason, in my view, is the rise in importing plants for sale in our garden centres. The sawfly entered the Netherlands, and as our world-famous British gardens depend so heavily on the Low Countries to supply the plants in British garden centres, it is not so surprising that this pest is newly arrived in Britain. So, too, is the insect which has infested our horse chestnuts, but it would be just as problematic in a cold phase. It survives more than twenty degrees of winter frost.

The threat of climate change is a convenient scare if, deep down, you hate lawns and lavish flower gardening. Is the weather really so savage in summer that the British lawn is now doomed and the only answer is something called St Augustine grass? Many gardeners will merely invest in pop-up sprinklers fed from their big receptacles for rain water. The RHS's professors claim in their study that 'as the climate progressively changes, a much greater challenge to gardeners will be to create the traditional English cottage garden'. They even suggest that lupins will become more difficult. I have never had better lupins than in the recent hot summers and as for the 'traditional' cottage garden, what exactly was it and what grew in it anyway?

As ever, there have been weather catastrophes, but catastrophes are not sound evidence of sustained change. The recent thunderclaps of wind and storms began to blow in 1987 and again in 1990 when they damaged well-established gardens, especially in the south of England. The National Trust can point to the loss of trees at Sheffield Park in Sussex, while others will think of the gales which ruined Tresco or opened up such lovely new vistas at Leonardslee. Were those storms connected with a warming of the British climate and a rising risk of floods? Again, Gilbert White puts the fears into a longer context. 'The year 1751 was one of the wettest years in the memory of man. There were constant storms and gluts of rain from 20 February to 20 May.' 1755 was 'a terrible winter for Earthquakes, Inundations and Tempests and continual Rains, with no frost worth mentioning'. In December 1761 'vast quantities of rain have fallen the autumn and winter through' and on 23 and 24 December there were 'vast rains and floods'. The 'climate of flooding' is not a modern innovation. It was already buffeting and soaking the mid eighteenth century.

What do the global warmers advise us to do? Their suggestions of myrtle hedges are a hollow joke in Moreton-in-Marsh or Much Wenlock. The RHS is seriously advising us to 'invest in water features and ponds – they will benefit wildlife'. Meanwhile, those who hate efficient, man-made fertilizers lose no chance of telling us that the increased risk of flooding raises the risk that such fertilizers will all be washed out of the soil and instead, we should heap on gravel and organic matter. How organic, though, is all this heaping? In the RHS garden at Hyde Hall in Essex, a newly installed 'dry garden' has already required '260 tonnes of gabbro'. In case you are unsure, gabbro is an igneous glacial rock which had to be transported from Scotland to Essex. The entire project reads to me like ecological rape, involving 800 tonnes of hard core, 460 cubic metres of imported soil and no end of 'crushed red granite'.

Thoughtful gardeners will continue to buy water butts to store their wasted rainwater and will give their gardens a backbone of plants which are totally hardy and capable of withstanding drought. Rock-hardy winter-flowering viburnums remain a wiser choice than mimosas. Spring-flowering hellebores are never killed by frosts and gales. Early flowering prunuses survive drought, cold and wind. Many narcissi flourish in the wild in glacial Russia and its neighbours. In summer, I have learned to trust border plants with chunky, water-retentive roots, the best varieties of day lilies, many of the yellow-flowered inulas and the excellent *Campanula lactiflora*, especially the deep blue 'Prichard's Variety' which arose on the fine nursery of Alan Bloom in Norfolk. At the edges of this backbone there has been a slight shift in reliable hardiness, which has brought many red- and yellow-flowered crocosmias, pink-flowered evergreen abelias and new agapanthuses within most British gardens' range. The reasons are better breeding and more experiment by gardeners, not a reliable shift to a plateau of warmer climate. When this backbone of plants is so solid and varied, who wants an incongruous palm tree, looking brown and increasingly ragged up its thick, ugly trunk? What we need is to dig in with the thousands of plants, still under-exploited, which flourish in the British climate, as ever one of extremes.

Faith, Hope and Charity

While experts debate the effects of a changing climate, gardeners can profit from a clear benefit. Mild winters in Britain are being kind to winter-flowering plants and I urge them on anyone starting a garden or trying to improve an old one. The traditional wisdom of garden designers was that winter-flowering shrubs and plants should be well represented in areas immediately surrounding the house and its doors. I agree. We stray much less farther afield in midwinter and it is heartening to see a pink-flowered viburnum, a winter-flowering cherry or a scented winter honeysuckle from the front door and its nearby windows. Winter honeysuckle is remarkably tough and will even flourish in odd corners beside the dustbins.

The festoons of flower on the yellow-flowered winter jasmine, *Jasminum nudiflorum*, are essential in any garden, and despite the plant's twiggy look in summer, it deserves a sunny place where its colour shows up best in midwinter. Its equals are the many forms of mahonia, another essential plant for beginners or hopeful improvers, and one which may help them to pull their ideas out of a rut. The mild weather nowadays allows the brightest mahonias to flower freely and the accompanying rain suits them too. Most of the family likes a wet season, one reason why such good mahonias are to be found in Ireland. The best known is *Mahonia japonica*, which tends to start flowering in mid-December, frost permitting. The flowers are scented of lily of the valley and open to a shade of acid yellow which is very appealing. The leaves are often a less glossy green than those on their near relations and can look rather drab in the off season or in dry shade, but at least they will grow and flower under light shade from tall trees. They are wonderful shrubs for under-planting a copse or bordering a little walk beneath trees, especially where the soil is unsuitable for azaleas. *Mahonia japonica* also remains one of the first choices for odd corners near the semi-shaded surrounds of the house. It is a joy to pick some of its scented flowers and enjoy them briefly in a heated room in January.

In many garden centres, japonica takes a back seat to the cleaner and shinier hybrid *Mahonia × media* 'Charity'. This excellent shrub has more leaves along its branches and flowers of a slightly brighter yellow than japonica's. It is extremely hardy and eventually spreads into a bush about eight feet high and wide. Great authorities praise it for its scent but it is not nearly as evident as japonica's brand. Its merits are its cleanness and tidiness, which endear it to shoppers who buy on impulse. 'Charity' was first picked out by Sir Eric Savill from a row of seedlings sent to Russell's nursery near Windlesham in Surrey. They originated from the great Slieve Donard nursery in Ireland, where they had been collected from the tall, slightly tender *Mahonia lomariifolia*, source of 'Charity's' fine evergreen leaves. Two other good seedlings were then raised from 'Charity' by Savill in the gardens of Windsor Great Park and were named 'Faith' and 'Hope'. 'Hope' disappeared altogether in 1964 after the election of a Labour government and 'Faith' has now dropped out of the *Plant Finder*.

'Charity' will still grow almost anywhere and, after five years, will give plenty of flowers and long leaves which reflect the light. I recommend it highly, and its traditional pairing in London with the big-fingered leaves of evergreen fatsia is a splendid match. The easy way to prolong the mahonia season is to choose one of the more recent crosses which were made between japonica and lomariifolia by the great plantsman Lionel Fortescue in Devon. The best is named *Mahonia × media* 'Buckland', and its spectacularly big clusters of flowers are held upright in a bright shade of yellow, usually opening in early February. On 'Buckland's' flowers the scent is elusive, although even here, some admirers detect it. Nonetheless, this variety is an excellent companion for japonica and 'Charity' because it comes later into flower.

I have two particular bits of mahonia wisdom. One is rare and the other surprised me when I first discovered it. The rare bit concerns a very small mahonia called *pumila* which is seldom seen and is unlike the winter flowerers I have mentioned. It is at home in the mountains of California and grows less than a foot high, showing off leaves that are either grey-green or green flushed slightly with a pale shade of brown. I bought this unusual variety about twenty years ago and have left it to make a life in a dry bed at the foot of an ancient medieval wall, conditions which its collectors tell us it likes in nature. It plainly likes them in Oxford and has spread healthily, flowering in late April in a strong shade of yellow. It is unusual and useful against weeds.

The surprising bit of wisdom is that you can cut the tall winter-flowering mahonias very hard into their old wood and do them a great service. As they age they tend to become leggy and show bare branches, but if you cut them very hard in early April, they will surprise you by throwing up young spiky leaves beside the cut and growing away all summer to flower freely again in the winter. Until you are forewarned, you would be unlikely to risk this treatment on a shrub which looks as if it would resent it.

Nancy in Paradise

As you take down your home's decorations after Christmas, perhaps you wonder, deep down, if you really have style. A few people have it, but many more never will. I know, because I knew the best of them, rightly revered as the supreme exponent of the English Country House style in decoration and furnishing. She would have rejected the label with an inimitable aside, but the eye, wit and elegance of Nancy Lancaster live on, as taste becomes more elusive and people even believe that it can be bought by the roll.

American-born Nancy Lancaster designed and decorated some of the most magical houses and rooms in England between the 1920s and the 1970s. She lived in them with a sequence of husbands, maintaining, not unjustly, that for the long haul she was a better chooser of butlers. She was born in Virginia, which remained the ideal landscape in her mind's eye, but 'English' style has often been most successful when conceived by people who are not English. Nancy combined smartness with comfort, everyday wear with wit and fun. She had a genius, as stylish Cecil Beaton observed, for 'offhand perfection'. It showed in her houses but also in her gardens and the smallest details of her dress and vocabulary.

Fortunately, photographs of her homes survive which are classics for designers or owners of a house with class. They run from the 1920s to the early 1990s, spanning Nancy's life which beautified so many special rooms. Her style enhanced the London business which she bought in 1944, Colefax and Fowler, a company which still survives. In it she linked up with John Fowler, her genius of a decorating partner, and together they were well described as the most unhappy unmarried couple in England. Such a marriage of talent and style flowed from their fertile disagreements.

Nancy's Virginian grandfather liked to remark that etiquette is for those who are not well born and fashion is for those who have no taste. Nancy exemplified his wisdom. Her first marriage was to the immensely rich and handsome Henry Field, grandson of the founder of the great Marshall Field store in Chicago. Henry died tragically within six months and Nancy then married the rich and cultivated Ronnie Tree. He was an ideal match for her talents and together they made interiors which were the acknowledged masterpieces of inter-war taste, above all in the great house at Ditchley in Oxfordshire where traces of Nancy's decoration survive. When they parted, Nancy told me how she went over by agreement to collect her remaining furniture from their house, in which her former husband was entertaining weekend guests with the young lady who duly became his wife. A Visitor's Book lay open in the hall and as Nancy left, without intruding on the party, she wrote in it in big letters, 'How is Puss getting on in my boots, then?' Puss was surprised to discover the message when she invited her first guests to sign their names in the book after lunch. Nancy, meanwhile, remarried briefly the owner of Kelmarsh in Northamptonshire, for the house as well as the company. When she left, she moved in 1954 to Haseley Court near Oxford, where she transformed an eighteenth-century house into yet another masterpiece, her final, happy home, and laid out gardens which were a fascinating tribute to her skill and eye.

More needs to be put on record about Nancy and this final garden. I know it, because I lived on the place in her last two years of ownership of the entire property and I gardened with her on many charmed days in the years when I was first writing columns on gardening. When she sold the main house she gave me many of her practical books on gardens and flowers. Gardening, she would say, is best done on your stomach, weeding with your teeth. We crawled and chewed, even when she was seventy-five, and almost every plant, its position and its partners in her garden remains imprinted on my mind.

By the time I knew her, Nancy had lived the grand life and spent money as freely as water from her garden hose. Nonetheless, she worked outdoors whenever she could, alarming my wife and myself by tugging the hose through the ground floor of the cottage which we rented from her and calling at six in the morning, 'When are you going to have babies or shall I come upstairs and show you how to do it?'

'I water in the mornings,' she told me, 'when I cannot sleep, so it is for you to see that I have not caught pneumonia when you wake up.' When we then had the babies, she compared the colour and texture of their cheeks in cold weather to ripening nectarines. Meanwhile, it was for me to accompany her with the long-handled pruners and to listen to the stream of memories, down-to-earth comments and questions which came at me from the middle of an over-sized deutzia or a favourite lilac which needed dead-heading.

'I have had the best of it,' she would tell me, 'when the best was worth having.' It still seemed pretty good to me, and I must adjust the published impression that the distinguished adviser Graham Thomas left a lasting imprint on Haseley's famous walled garden. Nancy respected his knowledge but was wary of his taste. It was not Graham Thomas who first taught her about many of the roses which she chose for her garden, from 'Mme de Sancy de Parabère' to stripy 'Leda' and climbing white 'Sombreuil'. She gave me a neglected book, *The Charm of Old Roses* by Nancy Steen, in which she had made copious marks and notes. It was her springboard, whereas there are many fewer such marks in her copies of Graham Thomas's classic works on old roses which she gave me too. Unwary readers of garden historians might think that her garden depended on two colour schemes, one of pink roses and after a crossing avenue, one of yellow roses. She certainly included those colours and when her sister complained that pink and orange did not go together, Nancy typically told her that, 'In time you'll begin to like anything with anything.' Green, she knew, helped harsh colours to blend, but I knew the garden at its height and, by then, the combination of pink and orange had long disappeared. It was replaced by a palette of a wider range which was Nancy's own.

How much I learnt from her, much more, even, than from my previous spell as a trainee gardener in Munich's botanical garden. Sometimes on winter evenings I still walk my mind round the details impressed on my memory: the Italian cypresses whose leaves smelt of paper in old books, the Canadian lilacs pulled over to make an arbour, the honeysuckles grown as standard trees, the patterns of silver *Artemisia splendens* and golden creeping jenny which evoked the pattern in a mosaic floor at Torcello in Venice's lagoon. She had a decorator's sense of staging and a boldness rooted in her own good taste. She grew big trees of the tender *Sparrmannia* and put them in cleverly shaped boxes which were painted in her favourite Confederate shade of grey. The plants had been grown from cuttings, she told me, first given her by Laurence Olivier. She trained huge plants of grey-leaved *Helichrysum petiolare* on wires in pots. In other pots she grew wisterias like trees, and for years afterwards I treasured the standard wisterias which she gave me. Everywhere there were rare roses which her eye had picked out as a match for Haseley's sandstone walls. I first learnt from her about the unusual rose 'Ash Wednesday' which has flowers of her favourite grey. She liked modern varieties too, the stronger pink 'Aloha' as a climber, tumbling yellow 'Golden Showers', the powder-scented 'Constance Spry'. Her main garden path was lined with the low box hedging which she had loved since her youth in Virginia. She acquired most of it for nothing when the National Trust threw it out from other gardens in a fit of labour-saving drabness. It was she who knew that old, leggy bits of box will grow bushily again if the bare bits are buried below the soil. She was always alert to practical wisdom.

Her fellow American, the admirable Lanning Roper, was an important source of advice in the garden's early years. Nancy was always a great magpie: 'I am not a decorator, I am a percolator.' Lanning Roper helped with ideas for her walled garden's planting after a first fallow year in which she cleaned it by growing potatoes all over the ground. He taught her to plant grey-leaved phlomis against the walls of the house or to plant *Campanula persicifolia* among bearded irises, but she taught me to love the stripy *Syringa vulgaris* 'Sensation', to cut Rosa mundi roses down to ground level after flowering or to interweave alstroemerias with silver-leaved *Senecio viravira*. My word, she made us laugh. One afternoon, two learned Oxford experts in Roman history came up to call from the village: she asked these confirmed bachelors how landowners had survived the farming depression of the 1880s. The more learned of the two replied, 'That is not my period', with a caution which young beginners abominate. 'Periods,' retorted Nancy, 'were the one thing I thought that professors like you never had.'

In the hot July of 1971 I used to walk in her heavenly garden in the cool of the day when the roses were falling everywhere and she was about to sell most of the ground she loved. She wrote at the time: 'Now it is gone, but life is a series of Grand National jumps. It is like the end of a party.' In her mid seventies she withdrew to the Coach House beside her former home and made yet another enchanting garden as if the party had merely changed its scale. She planted evergreen yews and clipped them, brilliantly, into a circular sofa with green arms. She contrasted them with a golden-leaved robinia and multiplied the regale lilies which she grew on canes in pots. 'Better at choosing butlers', she was sustained by her last choice, Fred, who learned how to make her whisky sour with the juice of fresh limes and how to remind her whom she had invited to lunch. As her years declined he would go out and record the chorus of early morning birdsong in her walled garden and play it to her while she lay in bed.

For me, the move from her house was like an expulsion from paradise. Others had shared this feeling. In the 1920s, a footman of hers remarked that 'Nancy sitting side-saddle on her horse before hunting, immaculate in her top hat and veil, is a picture I shall take to the grave with me and if afterwards I see her looking the same I shall know I am in heaven.' So shall I; but meanwhile, I look back with total recall on the garden which closed behind us. Over it stands an angel with a flaming sword, turning this way and that, but not because its lady owner had eaten its forbidden fruits. With characteristic Virginian wit, Nancy once sent a photo home to America, showing herself in a magnificent evening dress. She wrote on the bottom, 'How we apples float . . .'

Scenting Winter

In warmer winters, my best shrub beside the house is the excellent sarcococca. It makes a neat evergreen edging which varies according to the form planted. The leaves shine, the plants grow anywhere and they flower profusely, scenting the entire approach to the front door. I bless the day, twelve years ago, when I planted them by the dozen. I now have a solid hedge, about three feet high, which is covered in scented flowers, asking to be picked and taken indoors. Not enough is said about the value of these early, hardy shrubs as decoration inside the house. Their popular American name is Christmas box, honouring their shiny green leaves and small flowers. One vase of sarcococca scents an entire room, saving the expense of buying throwaway lilies.

I do not regret the form I chose. *Sarcococca confusa* is distinguished by its modest height, pointed leaves and black berries. Eventually, it might grow up to five feet but I clip my plants hard after flowering and find that a limit to their height increases their width. The smallest of the sarcococcas is *hookeriana humilis*, which grows about a foot tall and is willing to spread by its own suckers. However, it does not have the berries of other varieties – black on *confusa* or red on *ruscifolia*. As these two varieties can be controlled by pruning, they are first choices for a difficult corner in a garden. They thrive in cities.

Gardeners are more familiar with the sweeter, sickly scent of the skimmia. Well used, it is another charming shrub, but its sex life has to be sorted out. Unless you mix a male with females, you will not get the best berries on the best forms. One male can cope with up to five females in its vicinity but I tend to plant smaller groups of three, two females to one male. Among the females, the most profuse crops of large red berries come from *japonica* 'Nymans', closely followed by 'Veitchii'. I pair them off with the male *japonica* 'Fragrans', which is less tall and should go in front of them. There are other possibilities but I am not so fond of the varieties with red-purple buds or leaves which go yellow-green. All skimmias will grow almost anywhere and respond to pruning and shaping. Unexpectedly, they root with extreme ease from cuttings taken in spring after flowering. They make the most obliging green mounds for awkward, shaded situations. They also pick well, especially when in berry.

The superb winter honeysuckle is in every way the skimmia's equal. It is so easy, so free-flowering and so powerfully scented that I cannot imagine living without it. It hides the sort of dustbin on wheels which our local council gave to its ratepayers as if to help the environment. My winter honeysuckle has helped it far more than their green plastic. There are two varieties, of which the earlier, *Lonicera* × *purpusii* 'Winter Beauty', is better. It retains many of its leaves in most winters and it bears small cream-white flowers which are scented with a slight sharpness to their sweet base. Familiarity has taught me two extra possibilities. You can prune 'Winter Beauty' as hard as you like so that its eventual height and width of five or six feet will never be a problem. When you prune it, you can take whole branches indoors, where they will last for weeks and be very cheering. The other variety, *L. fragrantissima*, is almost as good as 'Winter Beauty' but it flowers later when it is less welcome.

The best of all early scents is a mimosa's and here, urban gardeners have the advantage. Mimosas never survive outdoors for long in chilly parts of Britain but they have become a spectacular sight in London. They are listed botanically as acacias and two of the best and hardiest sights are the pretty blue-green leaves of *Acacia baileyana* and the clusters of yellow flowers on *Acacia pravissima*, whose shoots tend to arch forwards. If you prefer mimosas with ball-shaped heads of flower in yellow bunches, ask for *Acacia dealbata*. Even in modern mild winters, I would still plant them with their backs against a south or west wall, remembering that they reach a considerable height very quickly. They soon race up to twelve feet or more and are an excellent choice for impatient urban house-owners. Their display in the garden is only part of their charm. Heads of mimosa are the most exquisite of scented plants for use indoors.

The only rival to these powerful scents is the exceptional winter-sweet, *Chimonanthus praecox*. Most of the forms available in the trade take a long while to flower, at least five years from the year of planting, but this slowness should not put you off. I prefer to see winter-sweets grown as free-standing bushes, which will develop up to seven feet high and wide with a favourable wall near them. If you train them against the wall itself, you cramp their style and lose the impact of the pale straw-yellow flowers, which do not show clearly against most colours of walling. A wait for up to seven years is infinitely worthwhile. All over the bare branches the flowers then give off such a heavy, spiced scent that not even a French scent-maker can recapture it. The flowers' pale, watery colouring remains remarkably robust during slight bursts of frost. If you shop carefully, you may even be lucky and alight on one of the quick-flowering forms. One such early flowerer was available recently through the nursery at Christopher Lloyd's home, Great Dixter in Sussex. Others are now reported, but they remain in short supply and are not yet available in general nurseries' lists.

Available but overlooked is the shrub with the sweetest sugary scent when it flowers in late February. *Ribes laurifolium* is overshadowed by its grander, red-flowered relations, but it remains a lovely plant, growing up to four feet tall and especially good when fixed against a low wall, even against one of those awkward low walls beneath a window. The flowers are pale green, noticed above all for their scent, and selected varieties are neater and even more generous in bud. 'Mrs Amy Doncaster' is still scarce, but commemorates a brilliant Hampshire gardener who died in 1995 when over a hundred. 'Rosemoor' is easier to find, but the basic *laurifolium* is just as beloved by bees.

A Hunter's Hand

Beyond the sarcococcas, I have finally achieved an aim which I announced nearly twenty-two years ago in the optimism of late youth. In the lower part of my garden, where the ground slopes gently downhill to a muddle of confused greenery, the goal was to imitate a formal pattern of avenues copied from great French gardens and known, four centuries ago, as a 'goose-foot' or *patte d'oie*. At the time the illustrator in the *Financial Times* provided a picture of geese heading outwards with strings in their beaks; twenty-three years later, have they run wild and flapped off into chaos? The answer is 'no', but at a cost.

I now have five clearly defined avenues at a height of more than twenty-five feet and a length of more than sixty yards. They could be called a goose-foot, or they could be compared to the five fingers on my right hand, whose outer edge has become splayed after a collision with the ground in Leicestershire during an excellent day's foxhunting. I prefer, therefore, to claim I have planted a Hunter's Hand. It is impressive, but every impression has its price.

Its composition was based on a guess. Others might have chosen tightly clipped horse chestnuts, trees which were used as an excellent formal hedge by the late David Hicks when he transferred his skills from interior to exterior design. If so, their hedges would now be brown, ruined in summer by the chestnut's new insect-predators. For my outer fingers, or alleys, I began by thinking of sorbus trees, one of which still survives as a memorial. It is impressive but I withdrew the other two avenues after hearing a lecture by an expert who predicted an epidemic of fireblight from the West country, targeted at the very variety which I had planted by the dozen. The withdrawal was wise, but for the wrong reason. The sorbus family is still waiting for this supposed attack from the West, but anyone who wants to imitate a goose-foot design should consider no more than two varieties of tree. I already had two. I had opted for a central avenue of hornbeam and outer avenues of an evergreen pear, *Pyrus calleryana* 'Chanticleer', chosen at random from a book. If a well-known garden centre had not supplied me with two back-up pears of the wrong variety, the outer avenues of 'Chanticleer', now four in all, would be perfect. Their combination with a central avenue of hornbeam is also good, but the hornbeam developed in unanticipated ways. Each tree was planted about three yards apart and between them I put a temporary filling of the scented *Philadelphus* 'Belle Étoile'. After twenty-two years, the philadelphuses are still only three feet high, hating the poor soil and the competition for water with the trees' roots. Last year, they were at their best, flowering freely near ground level before the trees put on a spurt in August and almost obliterated the light.

The downside is unexpected. In late April, the new leaves on all these trees open by the thousand in shades of fresh vivid green. They look unacceptably hectic in the middle distance until they mature and tone down. I had never expected the garden to be over-greened in this way. The visual counterweight should be strong red flowers, best found in oriental poppies or a vigorous Darwin tulip called 'Oxford', but they struggle to compete because the trees have matured, drying and shading the soil.

Before this excessively green phase, the pears flower so prolifically in early spring that at night they add an extra pale dimension to the light of the moon. Life with 'Chanticleer' pears is never dull. They lose their leaves very late in the year, and turn a brilliant shade of ruby, like an ageing professor after dinner, in a 'fall' which is often delayed until early December. Individually, the trees are stiff and upright in habit, but in groups they respond excellently to light clipping and will branch sideways into a continuous avenue if they are planted at intervals of three yards. Their best phase is from late July until November, when they have toned down and developed a charming, glossy sheen on their plain green leaves. Accept no substitutes for the 'Chanticleer' form of pear tree and enjoy watching its lower trunk swell with age, like the lower leg of a hard-worked horse.

My hornbeams are the regular *Carpinus betulus* 'Fastigiata', which is said in books to have an upright, fastigiate growth. In a way it does, but only after developing too much of a middle-aged spread. I have had to clip hard to keep the hornbeams upright and stop the width of bulge which develops in old specimens on roadsides. Nowadays, there is a truly upright hornbeam, *Carpinus betulus* 'Columnaris', which grows more slowly and would be more manageable. My original supplier, Landford Trees at Landford Lodge, Salisbury, Wiltshire, offers both varieties nowadays, but the choice was not available in 1987.

The formal patterns of these avenues look their best on ground which slopes gently away from the viewer so that they can be surveyed from a higher point. Maintenance was simple in the early stages. As I am not a believer in the organic fantasy, I made free and healthy use of weedkillers based on glyphosate, which are safe to apply between young trees because they are inactive when they fall on soil, not directly on leaves. The main commodities needed were patience and stability. It takes at least ten years for the effect of an avenue to develop and then you must allow time to cope with it. I fear I have now created a monster I cannot control. I am not willing to go up a ladder which is balanced on a fragile pear tree in order to cut a regular line for each avenue at a height of more than twenty feet. The more the trees are clipped on their sides, however, the more they grow up to the sky. The attempt to level them off has been the long-running drama of the past two summers and almost any equipment available for hire has a drawback in this situation. It is either so large that it squashes the intervening garden, or it refuses to work on a slope. I have come to rely on two expert tree-cutters whose jeep draws an ascending, powered platform for use among the central hornbeams.

On paper it may sound simple, but the hoist tends to sink into the ground in wet weather and the entire job takes a week, once every eighteen months. It is not cheap and for the workmen it is not pleasant. I am not giving up, because a *patte d'oie* or Hunter's Hand brings months of developing beauty and only a brief bout of spring frenzy. It is not an asset for anyone's old age and it leaves me wondering how our unmechanical Georgian ancestors cut the high hedges in their avenues so neatly. At Chiswick House or Versailles, they did not have a mechanical platform, but neither did they have officials for health and safety. When labour was cheap, standards of risk and expendability were ominously cheaper too.

A Year's Itinerary

While I wait for the first flower-buds on my avenues of pears I ask myself on cold wet days, if money and distance were not obstacles, what would be a good itinerary for a garden visitor in each month of the year? Fortunately I can think of so many different itineraries. They would begin in January and February with the sub-tropical gardens at Abbotsbury, near Weymouth, Dorset, a favoured site which has fine shrubs in flower throughout the early months. Maintained by the Ilchester Estate, the garden draws on more than a hundred years of intelligent planting, little of which we can grow in our colder gardens. I would also visit the Eric Young Orchid Foundation on Jersey, which deserves its prominent place on the island's postage stamps. The standards of flower and cultivation in this collection are unsurpassed, and if you coincide with the slight scent which rises from its slipper orchids, the paphiopedilums, under glass in early February, you enter paradise in your imagination. The next stop would be Cornwall. In our warmer winters the gardens at Caerhays near St Austell tend to hit their peak as early as mid-March. They remain the most stunning sight in the exotic world of magnolias, camellias and rhododendrons, because they include so many of the original collections from the Far East. They are also the home of many of the williamsii hybrid camellias, which have transformed the spring season of sheltered urban gardens. Despite the sea winds, a visit is unforgettable. On the return journey you should drop in at Trewithen, the masterly Cornish garden of the late George Johnstone, whose central walkways show the loveliest displays of camellias and mature rhododendrons.

In April, the destination would have to be Sissinghurst Castle in

Kent. Repetition never stales the impression of the spring flowers in the section of the garden which Harold Nicolson regarded as his 'life's work'. In mid-April, you can admire the mixtures of so many small spring bulbs in the little beds beneath his long walk of pleached limes. You can then go on to the superb clumps of white trilliums near the hazel trees, an area which used to be bedded out with polyanthus. In April, the coach parties, too, are fewer.

Further afield, I would hunt out the enchanting garden at Castello in Florence which is accessible from the city on a number 28 bus. It is open only in the mornings, but is closed on Mondays. Much of the enlarged plan which was laid here in the sixteenth century by the Medici family has vanished nowadays, but the box parterre has charm and the wide range of lemon trees in their terracotta pots are a memorable sight in their shelter-house in April. In the warm greenhouse on the east of the garden, the most sweetly scented variety of tender white jasmine was first cultivated. Nowadays, azaleas and some showy peonies brighten up the place, too, but it remains evocative and under-visited.

In May, my first choice is the Botanischer Garten in Munich, accessible by the city's number 2 tram to Nymphenburg. By mid-May, its enormous alpine garden is a mass of flowers on almost every outcrop of rock and in the main garden the central beds show a brilliant scattering of tulips and bedding in colours which we would not always risk in England. It remains the outstanding botanical garden in continental Europe. For a wilder note, my trail turns south to the matchless garden of Ninfa, two hours' drive to the south-west of Rome, when it is dripping with wisteria and the purple-blue flowers on its paulownias. American, English and Italian taste met as nowhere else here in the Caetani and Howard families across nearly a hundred years and made a garden among the ruined buildings of a medieval Italian township. Helped by the site's constant springs of water, it is still Italy's jewel.

In the third week of May, you may be beginning to dread the prospect of another Chelsea Flower Show. If so, prepare for it at the exquisite garden of Bagatelle in Paris, within easy reach of the city's centre and the Bois de Boulogne by metro and then a number 246 bus. From about 20 May onwards, the iris garden here is beautiful and already, the early roses will be bursting into flower while the fine

Japanese peonies are open, too, on the far side of the house, leading down to the lake.

I recommend that you stay at home in June and celebrate, perhaps, with a visit to the impressive long borders at New College, Oxford, open every afternoon. As I plant and oversee them, I like to think they are a comfort to the suffering souls in the college while they sit their final exams. By late June, you should move on to Hampshire where the pair of long herbaceous borders at Bramdean House, near Alresford, mirror each other's colours and contents. They show you that much 'modernist' gardening is uglier and more boring than traditional herbaceous planting in the classic style. From mid-June onwards you should also go up to the great garden on the edge of the Cotswolds, Kiftsgate Court in Gloucestershire. Now in the third generation of the same family, it has been raised to even higher levels of sensitive planting by Anne and Johnny Chambers. The alstroemerias flower while the Chinese deutzias are setting buds in the formal Pool Garden. *Campanula latiloba* 'Highcliffe Variety' persists under tall trees, the Rosa mundi rose-hedge is magnificent and the rampant Kiftsgate rose is in full white flower on overpowering branches which run high up the trees and cover a width of hundreds of yards. This rose is a spectacle to be admired, but not imitated in gardens with less space for its aggressive vigour.

In July, I would go off to my favourite small garden, Helen Dillon's walled garden at Sandford Road in the Ranelagh district of Dublin. At that season her drooping dieramas are at their best and her two differently coloured borders complement each other down the length of what used to be the Dillons' perfect lawn. Go and see what the acknowledged queen of small hardy plants has done to her garden's grassy axis. At every turn, the small groupings of plants here are works of genius, beautifully grown and understood.

In August, I would choose the peaceful atmosphere and neat formality of Iford Manor near Bradford-on-Avon in Wiltshire, the Italianate garden of the thoughtful Edwardian architect Harold Peto, which I describe in more detail in my Autumn section. In the third week of September, I would go to the great sanctuary of the Michaelmas daisy, the Picton Garden at Old Court Nurseries, Colwall, to the south of Great

Malvern. Its one-and-a-half acres are densely planted with autumn flowers, and on Michaelmas Day the huge sweeps of asters and accompanying daisies and rudbeckias provoke immediate envy. They are a brilliant example of a wild style of planting which is not confined to short-lived British wildflowers or stale shades of pink and mauve.

In October I am sure the trail ought to lead across to America to Vermont, but I know its maple forests only from television and cannot suggest more than a drive down the highways which are best known for the fall. In England, meanwhile, I am content to visit the changing colours at Westonbirt Arboretum in Gloucestershire. In November, the route bends back to the RHS garden at Wisley in Surrey to see the greenhouse-displays of formally trained chrysanthemums which tumble on wires in the shapes of sprays and fountains. They set the standards for all growers who have the energy to fight off whitefly in a cool chrysanthemum-greenhouse.

December is in no way a postscript. In the weeks before and after Christmas, the spectacular gardens at Longwood in Pennsylvania remain the most brilliant display of indoor plants and exterior lighting in the world. Longwood is twelve miles north of Wilmington, Delaware, and although it has the resources of the Dupont Foundation to support it, it sets a yearly example which justifies every cent of the $20 million expense. It reminds us that darkness is not universal in winter in the world of gardening. In its East and Main Conservatories the bedding-out for Christmas is a thoughtful revelation. Multi-coloured cyclamen and unusually coloured poinsettias are massed with brilliantly unseasonal white snapdragons, the rare plume-flowered *Euphorbia fulgens* and an enchanting heather, I promise, called *Erica canaliculata* with tiny white flowers. Running through them is one of the garden's hallmarks, the spikes of true blue flowers on lovely *Plectranthus thyrsoideus*, not displayed in British botanical gardening. From the showers of wild orchids to the Brazilian plantings of the great Burle Marx, Longwood is the pinnacle of practical, artistic gardening.

If you follow this trail, you will be horticulturally broadened and financially stretched. Alternatively, you could make these visits one by one over the next few years. Meanwhile, I will have regrouped and, like you, come up with another twelve which are irresistible too.

I Spy a Hyena

For those of us who stay at home, heavy snowfalls are increasingly rare in British gardeners' experience of late winter. When one hit our gardens recently, it gave them a fortnight of night-time visibility, like an x-ray in reverse. For the first time I saw what really goes on in my garden after midnight. I did not like the look of it at all.

The action began sweetly and for the first two days I felt sentimental. In the snow on the lawn two unidentified animals, surely fluffy and furry, were imprinting their uninvited tracks. From opposite ends of the garden they drew irresistibly closer. They described two little circles and overlapped under one of the garden arches on which a white-flowered wisteria flowers in May. I pictured two happy rabbits taking time off work because snow had blocked their usual commute to their feeding-grounds. I even imagined wisteria as the animal equivalent of mistletoe under which the two of them had stopped and lovingly brushed whiskers.

On the third day there were yet more signs of these visitors. Snowed into my home, I went out in gumboots to investigate and I need only say here that it seemed they had not stopped at kissing. Feeling slightly envious, I trudged back indoors. I expected that the evening would see a snow-melt and that the cumbersome traces of my gumboots among the lovers' footprints would have disappeared by dawn. Instead, snow fell so deeply that even a buck rabbit abandoned the joy of sex in a snowdrift.

The snowfall glistened so crisply on the following day that I should have brushed it off my ceanothus. I did not, because I wanted to see another print-out in white of the garden's lovelife without human footprints to spoil it. In my mind's eye I remembered the classic Alfred Hitchcock film *Rear Window*. Signs of disturbance in the garden alerted Hitchcock's onlooker to a crime in his backyard. I would be a front-window detective on the morning after, not a voyeur from the rear.

The night-time duly saw some action but not of the kind I expected. Tracks proliferated from all directions and love had evidently taken flight. There were two hares, three rabbits, some impudent foxes, and the tracks to and fro of a badger. A cluster of paw-prints converged on streaks of blood and feathers where the corpse of a pigeon had been ripped open. No respect had been shown to the flowerbeds. A gang of beasts had run straight through my Michaelmas daisies and had relieved themselves on my favourite *Cistus × laxus* 'Snow White'. Are our gardens treated in this way every night while gardeners are peacefully asleep? These tracks make a nonsense of the Royal Horticultural Society's promotion of the garden as a 'haven' for wildlife. I want plants in my garden, not bloody-minded badgers, and I do not see how a haven is the right description for a space in which wildlife rips its fellow members to bits. Suspicions intensified when I bent down on one knee and started to analyse the tracks. Badgers are unmistakable and after fifty years of chasing foxes I am not going to be deceived about them. The problem was a deep-clawed imprint. It was not a cuddly squirrel. It had led the assault on the pigeon and had dragged the carcase away from the crime. I sketched the footprint on an old seed packet and went indoors to check in a book.

It was no use looking in books about Winnie-the-Pooh. It was certainly not a Wizzle and the claws ruled out a Woozle. From long ago I have a chart called *I-Spy Tracks*, a relic of the days in newspaper history when Big Chief I-Spy set competitions from his wigwam in central London and asked for them to be solved by young readers like myself. Big Chief I-Spy agreed with me that the claws were not a badger's. The near-perfect fit was a hyena.

I know you do not believe that hyenas live in the Cotswolds. Are you sure? Yellow-eyed big cats have been sighted in Wales around Lampeter and nobody knows what they are. Mad enthusiasts are trying to introduce beavers into the north of Britain. Sadists want to re-establish wolves in Northumberland. One of my Oxford colleagues even wants to release lynxes to kill off competing animals in the Home Counties. Has a human scientist already let out a hyena? Sabre-toothed hyenas were only too active in prehistoric Somerset, because their bones have been found in the caves at Wookey Hole. In the 1820s Oxford's Reader in Geology, the thoughtful William Buckland, used to mesmerize his undergraduates by waving the bone of a hyena to illustrate his lectures. Kirkdale Cave in Yorkshire had just been opened and found to contain teeth and bones which Buckland recognized as relics of elephants, rhinoceroses, hippos and hyenas. Biblicists argued that the animals had been sheltering from God's Flood, but Buckland pointed to the toothmarks on many of the bones. They belonged, he argued, to a den of antediluvian hyenas who had dined on the beasts in the cave. Where are those hungry hyenas nowadays? Only the print-out of a rare snowfall allows us to see what animal games go on after midnight. Hyenas may well hide by day and come out at night when badgers invite them to a cocktail party with canapés dipped in blood. With due respect to the RHS, I do not want a haven for hyenas. I want happy gentians and my own spinach.

As the light faded I was ever so slightly nervous inside my barricaded home. I listened to Prime Minister's Question Time on the radio and I think the exchanges must have drifted into my dreams. After dawn I woke to find yet more claw-tracks and churned snow, two more headless pigeons and a trail of cloven hoofprints on top of the best agapanthus. They had arrived in the week of the stimulus package for failing financiers. Evidently, the animal kingdom had taken a stimulus package of its own. What, I wondered, are the political affiliations of these animal offenders? It may have been Prime Minister's Questions which caused me to pose this problem, but I found myself recalling a classic exchange in the first of those parliamentary debates about 'hunting with dogs'. The late Nicholas Ridley began it with a chilling description to the House of Commons of a stoat in his Tewkesbury constituency. Ridley had witnessed it, he told them, mesmerizing a rabbit and then shredding it to pieces in cold blood. His conclusion was that animals of such brutality should be hunted without scruple. He was answered from the far left by Tony Benn, congratulating Ridley, a Thatcherite apostle of jungle law in economics, for realizing at last that the jungle needed regulation.

There is no regulation in my garden after midnight and plainly the law of the jungle lives on. My academic colleagues in Oxford liked to equate Margaret Thatcher with C. S. Lewis's White Queen, ruling in Narnia in a realm of frozen snow. If you have been wondering where Thatcherites have gone in the latest economic crisis, the answer is they are out there in the wilderness, celebrating in our garden-havens when a snowfall reminds them of their Queen's old days. I know you still find the hyena hard to credit. Admittedly, Big Chief I-Spy's chart was printed before the muntjak was known in British gardens and its hoofprints may need to be taken into account. Meanwhile, I am sticking to my hyena theory, and a right-wing hyena at that. Naturally it is laughing the whole way to the nearest unregulated bank.

On the Dutch Dealing Floor

During the animal activities of this early February, cut flowers sent me on a different track. After flowering for four incredible weeks since Christmas, the pollen and petals of my pale pink lilies at last collapsed and went from their vase to a well-earned grave. Where do these prolonged performers come from? I discreetly asked their provider and traced them back to their source.

The trail took me at 6.30 a.m. through driving rain to the heart of Europe's floral industry, the sheds at Aalsmeer in Holland. They are just down the road from Amsterdam's Schiphol airport and are not a usual haunt for an Oxford don who has not yet had a cooked breakfast. Aalsmeer is the biggest warehouse area in Holland, with a floor space of more than a million square yards, criss-crossed by ten miles of railway lines under cover. It supplies many of the cut flowers which in Britain we believe to be fresh. It makes Covent Garden Market look like a secondary parasite.

Ever alert to the problems of a female readership, I believe I have hit on the perfect solution for grumbling husbands. Suppose you are married to an over-age broker, the sort of man who is still unable to accept the Big Bang, that shockwave which eliminated face-to-face dealing on the floor of the old London Stock Exchange and the lunch hours which followed with his male friends. What can you do with him when, deep down, he is still expecting you to cook him a three-course lunch as graciously as the debutantes who used to enliven his London office? Here is the answer. Enrol him in a crash course in the Dutch language and pack him off to Aalsmeer.

He has no idea what heaven awaits him. There are eight old-fashioned dealing rooms, each with 200 traders who long to test their wits against new arrivals. They will give him his own personal red and yellow button and expect him to revive his skills of mental arithmetic without use of the dreaded computer. Every plant and flower on offer is propelled through the dealing room on a sort of adult train set. He can bid for the coaches one by one, placing his bets according to a fast-moving clock whose face is so big that even middle-aged eyes behind spectacles can make out the numbers. They will look bewildering at first, but he will soon realize that the numbers on the lower right refer to the cut flowers' quality and length of stem. The middle bands give the numbers in each lot and a rapidly travelling light marks the bidding price by zooming round the face of the clock.

There is one further advantage. The prices are agreed like the prices of investments when one tries to sell them by telephone. They go downwards, not upwards. At Aalsmeer, if he misses the first press of the button, he will get a second chance. Quite often the price is still falling and he will gain by having made his mistake. No smart little jobber will then bid him up to teach him a lesson. If he presses the wrong button and buys a load of flowers which he does not want, he will have a big bunch of Valentines to take home for the wives and girlfriends in his flirtatious history.

I now come to the part which he will find irresistible. Every single dealer in each of the clock-rooms is a man. Two women, Riet, say, and Anya, stand down on the stage, pointing out the loads on offer to the males in the seats above. Most of the bidders are early-to-middle-aged Dutchmen who seem to be doing almost nothing. After doing it they go out into the waiting room and smoke like chimneys.

Prices tend to stabilize after the first hour, and from 8 a.m. until 11 a.m. the dealings in cut flowers run within an established range of day-trading, settling into limits for which new bidders are not wholly responsible. Do not underestimate the scale of the operation, although entry is for dealers only. They pay €650 for a yearly card after proving the existence of a cash-pile in their bank accounts, and in a single morning they help about 21 million flowers and pot plants to find new owners. The Aalsmeer market recently merged with its only equal, Flora Holland. The merger began in 2008 and the joint venture now turns over the huge sum of €4 billion of perishable stock.

Naturally, some of it is hideous. As I watched, truckloads of my worst floral enemies were being sold off at prices between €0.29 and €0.24 per stem. If you are buying in thousands, those marginal points make a difference. On stage, Anya and Riet point to truckloads of sea lavender and a merry sort of sunflower called *Helianthus* 'Sunrich'. They sell in 20 seconds and the next carriage-load is full of *Solidago* 'Tara Gold'. From the Netherlands, the British import about €650 million worth of cut flowers each year, but even so, they are beaten by the insatiable Swiss, Norwegians and Austrians. Perhaps the British total should be increased by adding all the flowers which our supermarkets fly in from Kenya, Uganda and Israel. Even so, there is no escaping the Dutch. Flowers come to Aalsmeer from these same sources, because Dutch growers are out there organizing the trade. More than 16,000 varieties pass through the Dutch sheds every year, and it is impressive how much of the stock at auction still originates in the Netherlands, where more than 6,000 growers specialize in cultivating it under glass.

In 1997, there were fantasy plans for a link by underground tunnels between the flower market and Schiphol airport so that flowers could travel even faster to and fro. This Dutch tunnel vision has never been realized. Meanwhile, like the Dutch, I hope the streamlined enterprise continues to thrive. The business is run as a cooperative, which would normally fill onlookers with foreboding, but the structure suits the Dutch temperament. It caters for yearly variations in profit and the likelihood of a small return on most years' turnover. About 3,000 members submit to careful controls of quality and pay transaction costs of about 5 per cent on the value of loads which are bought by their buzzers. This flower market is the least promising business for a private equity buy-out, but in confidential rooms I saw the secrets which keep it ahead of rivals in China or Dubai. Seventy quality inspectors grade and assure the classing of all the goods which go up on the clock. Any new variety must be submitted by its grower for testing before stock is auctioned. On long benches I saw specimen vases of the new cut flowers of the future which were being controlled at room temperatures and observed for their ability to persist. Now-adays, I found with regret, cut-flower roses have to be bred without scent if they are to last long enough for their demanding clients indoors. I can well understand why my Dutch-auctioned lilies persist for four weeks in water. Breeders and judges have been striving to establish such long-lasting varieties.

Would I consider premature retirement to one of the floral floors? I hate an early start and I hate cigarette smoke. I will stay put because I like the mixed smiles of male and female pupils beneath the non-commercial clock of an Oxford library.

Wild on the Broadwalk

Like those dealers in the Dutch market, we all divide our lives into separate compartments. In our biographical cabinets, one drawer is for family and others for friends; one for facts, now partly forgotten, and others for fantasies, perhaps more than we recognize. What happens if we break down the barriers which keep the compartments apart? We have heard so much about joined-up government, and yet the results seem even more detached from reality. What about joined-up living?

In 2003 I joined up three of the least-related compartments in my personal space. They are not an obvious unity. One is gardening, especially in botanical gardens. Another is horses, especially with stirrups, and the third is my lifelong fascination with the history of Alexander the Great. In sweaty Thailand, I galloped wildly on horseback for Alexander's sake through a big botanical garden, unlisted and unrecognized by Britain's RHS. I have not lost my grip on reality. It truly happened, thanks to that queen of illusion, a motion picture for the big screen. First in Morocco, and finally in Thailand, I played my part in Alexander's cavalry, loyal to my superstar Colin Farrell, under the guidance of our god Dionysus, the inimitable Oliver Stone, director of the epic Alexander film.

I doubt if any other gardening columnist has left hoof-prints among the trees of a botanical forest. They have certainly never made them to camera, surrounded by the cavalry of the King of Thailand. Our location was described in my script as 'jungle', but Dionysus never told me that his jungle would be man-made and that he was asking me to attack an enemy concealed by the work of 150 gardeners who had been planting and watering the venue for three months. I shared in the attack from the back of a horse, first a black one, then a chestnut one, complete with leathery horse-blankets made from the hide of an 'upholstery cow'. We charged in the Phukae Botanic Garden, a gigantic park some sixty miles outside Bangkok.

On days of duty, I would gallop into battle for my squadron leader Hephaestion, while his beloved Alexander urged us onwards for the sake of immortal glory. I detest almost every form of ornamental grass, but as our squadron waited to career through the woods, workers with mattocks and pitchforks bedded clumps of chunky grasses along our route to make its course seem even more rough and natural. While stuntmen bumped into the tree trunks, I had time to check the botanical labels which were whizzing past my horse's bridle on the intervening branches. In Thailand, January is the dry season, but the botany of the Phukae garden has a scope and range which leave my expertise floundering. Specimens with names like spondias and diospyros mean nothing to an English provincial mind. Even if you have seen a schleichera in leaf, I bet you have never galloped through one so that the tips of its branches brush your silvered cavalry helmet.

Western gardeners know nothing about this extraordinary botanical garden. In the Saraburi province, it is a vast expanse of state-maintained greenery, divided in two by a busy out-of-town road. On one side, I explored on foot its huge expanse of clipped box topiary, in which grey boulders were arranged like units in an oriental army. In the intervening spaces there was nothing but pine trees and vivid bougainvilleas. Elsewhere I recognized a tamarind tree, but the rest of the planting baffled me, not least because a cohort of busy Thai ladies continued to spray it with hoses while failing to grasp my questions in sign language. The only guide to this side of the garden is a big green model at its entrance which shows acres of unnamed treetops. Across the road, however, the trees in the other section are arranged in orderly botanical families, ranging from Ebonies to Guttiferous and Leguminous plants. Our army's base camp was beside the section of Euphorbias, the family whose plants squirted juice into the eyes of Alexander's horses in the ancient Iranian desert and rendered them blind. My black cavalry charger kept his head up and I think from the map that we had to gallop in the section which the garden-model called Dilleniaceae.

Perhaps I will now be asked to gallop down the Broad Walk in Kew Gardens. I am not sure that I recommend a close exploration of a jungle imported for Hollywood. The danger is not that the green bananas and accompanying bamboos will begin to turn brown when the season warms up. It is that their jungle was the cover for an array of elephants, equipped with tusk-extensions and ferocious female mahouts. The plants in the man-made jungle had been chosen to be elephant-compatible so that the beasts would not uproot and eat them on their first battle-charge. Instead, they sheltered in its canopy of vivid green until they emerged towards our horses and dared us to take them on.

The film shows some of the results, but it does not show the botanical labelling. Nor does it show how a horse gallops off to the left when an elephant begins to charge it. It also does not show a thoughtful gardener's fury in battle. On flights to Thailand, the airlines show a film to passengers about animals in films, entitled *Wild on Set*. It is now obsolete. It has nothing about the latest wild animal, a historian on horseback, charging through trees which he cannot recognize despite fifty years of English gardening.

The Lettuce Farm Palace

More than thirty years before this cavalry service in a Thai botanical forest, I had visited Thailand and reported on my visits round private Bangkok gardens. I met and learned from their presiding spirit, the expatriate American William Warren, who held the honoured position of gardening columnist on the *Bangkok World* newspaper. My visit fell in Thailand's rainy season and for much of the day my wife and I were marooned in a small hotel room, at whose bare wooden table I wrote my account of the crowning victory against elephants which was won by Alexander the Great in north-west India. In the afternoons, I would meet with Thailand's most perceptive gardener, Pimsai Amranand, sadly now dead from a random attack in her house by an armed intruder. My text on Alexander has been more fortunate. It played a part in the filming of *Alexander*, for whose sake I returned to Bangkok to re-enact the very elephant-battle which I had written up in the city.

After my first visit I remembered how my garden hosts had regretted that it had not been possible to meet Thailand's most distinguished gardener, a princess of the royal house. On my return visit, Alexander's filming schedule took a break on a Sunday and the cavalrymen were left to amuse themselves. I chose a trip to the first place which my guidebook to Bangkok mentioned as a garden with a 'tranquil retreat'. Its name was Wang Suan Phakkat, which means the Lettuce Farm Palace. The one keen gardener in the film production was the set decorator, whose last assignment had been on *Seven Years in Tibet*. Together, we set off for three hours in a Lettuce Farm.

If I believed in the gods, I might think that I was being guided. Here

I had returned, fighting for a film-army in the very battle whose history I had first written up in Thailand. Here I was, too, pushing open the gate of what turned out to be the lovingly tended garden of the late Princess Chumbhot, the princess whom I had missed on my previous visit. The Lettuce Farm Palace has a heartening origin. In 1932, the Thai royal family was deposed and the family members had to go into exile. Among them was the young Princess Chumbhot, who left with her parents for England and stayed there for the next five years. Most of the family's properties were taken away from them, and when the surviving family members returned to Bangkok, they chose to reside on ground surrounded by simple allotments, a virgin site. They bought a few of the neighbouring plots and over the years they developed their ordinary surroundings into the separate houses which now cluster around their Lettuce Farm residence. Their plot of ground received a pavilion from a temple site in the countryside, and around it four groups of traditional houses became filled with items from the royal collection and relics of the prince's passion for music. There was also a garden in which the young Princess Chumbhot decided to work with her own hands.

Among the allotments on a Bangkok lane, the influence of gardening seen in England has left an unexpected mark. During her exile in England, the princess had learnt that English gardens like to show off their flowers and trees. Her love of flowering plants blossomed and during the next forty years she assembled a variety of trees, shrubs and courtyard gardens in Bangkok which are still a credit to her taste. She had a Far Eastern love of rocks and artistically arranged stones. She planted brilliant water lilies in tubs. She imported flowering specimens which Thai gardeners had never seen. Each of her visits abroad led to an addition to her garden's collection. I found myself struggling with botanical families which I had never encountered before. Quassia is a striking plant with scarlet spikes of flower, and if only the weather in Oxford was warmer, I would cherish an ochua with rounded cream-yellow flowers.

By a roundabout route, I had returned to the missing piece of my previous visit to Bangkok. What was the princess like? In the small accompanying museum, I found the final piece in the jigsaw, an appreciation of her by my previous host in Thailand, the gardening columnist of the *Bangkok World*. William Warren emphasized how she worked in the garden herself and knew and planted everything in it. She would call herself, laughingly, the simple housewife, Mrs Wigg of the Cabbage Patch. There was nothing of the Castle of Mey about her or the arm's-length extravagance of England's Queen Mother. In William Warren's view, the princess resented the lack of education which had befallen her as a Thai princess. She corrected it by constant reading, travelling and talking. In 1976, Bangkok was shaken by a student revolution which was repressed very forcefully by the police. William Warren remembered calling on the princess in her garden house that afternoon and finding her weeping over a tin of Iranian caviar. As she watched the events unfolding on television, she exclaimed through her tears: 'Idiots, dumb idiots.' He then realized that she was referring to the police.

From palace to cabbage patch, the princess's route turned out to be one of enlightenment. Exile turned her to gardening, England inspired her and she returned to lay out the neatest town garden in a Bangkok setting which would have worn down a less flexible mind. If we had met thirty years before, I might perhaps have recognized orchids like *Cymbidium simulans*, which is still growing in her trees. It would have been fun to learn about the blue-flowered eranthemum and to discuss the very different art with which she arranged her personal rock garden, so different to ours in the English tradition.

Some twenty-five years after her death, the gardens are still open daily from 9 a.m. to 4 p.m. If you can decipher Bangkok's number 3 bus, it stops right outside the gate. There are always good things in flower, but I doubt if you will recognize more of them than I could. You will certainly not recognize a wonderful yellow-flowered variety of the pink trumpet tree, which is otherwise known as tabebuia. Only a week before Princess Chumbhot died, she was delighted by the flowering of this yellow beauty. It was the only one known in a gardener's care. As my two trips to Bangkok joined up and came full circle, I honoured the thoughtful gardener who transferred herself from a throne-room to a simple allotment and left a permanent mark of beauty on her world.

Christopher Lloyd

For even more years than Bangkok and its elusive princess, a great fellow garden writer has been a guiding force in my life. In his absence I share with many gardeners the sense that there is a hole in the mixed border of our lives. Christopher Lloyd died in February 2006 after nearly eighty years of gardening. He was the acknowledged king of garden writers and one of the most influential masters of practical gardening in all its forms. He was the most thoughtful of gardeners and his thoughts had a frequent edge to them.

Lloyd's Sussex garden at Great Dixter remains a living testimony to his distinctive eye and tireless mind. He wrote profusely, delighting weekly readers of *Country Life* magazine for more than forty years. His admirers multiplied in the last twenty years of his life, as he set an inspiring example of the irrelevance of 'retirement' to serious human beings. Like the ancient wise man Solon, Christopher grew old, 'always learning much'. He delighted in the company of the young and made his home an open house for younger visitors, whatever their background, if they loved plants and nature. He even became an American icon, a status reinforced by his own visits to the States and his lucid, but unpredictable, lectures.

He was a distinctive person formed at a distinctive time and his death left me with a sense that one of the last titans in the field has gone. People always think that, a younger colleague consoled me, when the masters of their earlier days have died. I do not think this view is correct. There were unrepeatable reasons why Christopher was a commanding example. His distinctive eye and style led to scores of distinctive anecdotes. I fielded or caused quite a few of them in my years as a writer on gardening.

Christopher Lloyd began with an advantage enjoyed by few gardeners nowadays. He lived throughout his life in the fine house in which he was born and so he never had to lay out a garden from scratch. One of the concerns of his later life was to keep this property together and pass it on through a complex web of family ownership. The main beneficiary was his niece, who then sold her part-share to a Trust backed by a big grant from the Heritage Lottery Fund, matched by funding from other sources. Nearby Dixter Farm has now been bought for teaching and the housing of students, and an extra car park is now available too. Christopher would be pleased, because he had capitalized on his fame for the sake of the garden's future, remaining both coy and amused by the results. In later life he auctioned superfluous items from Dixter and made himself inconspicuous in his gardening clothes in the garden during the sale. Nonetheless he was not displeased that even his trowel, though almost defunct, went to an American buyer for £200.

Christopher was born in 1921 and was brought up, the youngest of six children, in a strict household. He rapidly found his life's work outdoors. His father, Nathaniel, was an able architect, and was very close to Sir Edwin Lutyens, whose designs were important for the Dixter house. His mother, the remarkable Daisy, makes sporadic appearances in Christopher's gardening books and left a lasting impression on his personality and outlook. He was twelve when his father died but he continued living with his mother until her death in 1972: there were moments of petulance, but their relations remained very close, central to each other's lives. Daisy had an independent spirit too. After a visit to Austria in her early years, she surprised surrounding society in Sussex by wearing an Austrian dirndl for much of her remaining life. Daisy was an extremely keen gardener and she recalled how her son soon began to work with her outdoors. At the age of seven he could name many plants in the garden. She and her husband were friends of the great Miss Jekyll and used to visit her famous Surrey garden where Christopher was presented to her as a keen boy-gardener. Inadvertently Miss Jekyll authorized him, commanding him to 'go on with the good work'. She gave Dixter four fine plants of the spiky *Yucca gloriosa* but his mother moved them away for fear that the pointed leaves might damage one of her children.

Christopher grew up to be extremely sharp himself. He benefited from a clear mind and a Cambridge education but he combined them with a practical devotion to gardening, not just to garden-watching. His classic book is *The Well-Tempered Garden*, still one of the fundamental texts for gardeners. The imperious designer Russell Page was one of those who remarked to me that it was a pity that it was a book by such an ill-tempered gardener. Nothing could be less true. Christopher was not bad-tempered. He was irreverent and mischievous but was always prepared to give credit where he owed it. In reply, he described Page's own admired book, *The Education of a Gardener*, as an education in arrogance, not gardening.

Visits by Christopher to one's own garden were unpredictable and were famous for leaving a sting behind. Eventually he paid a visit to one of the few practising gardeners who is a match for him, Helen Dillon in Dublin. She let him go out alone into her stunning garden at the back of her town house in Sandford Road and watched while he went down on one knee, ignored its brilliant planting and merely looked over the garden wall. When he came inside, he told her: 'Helen, your neighbour has a very interesting kind of holm oak.'

She was not deterred: 'Christopher,' she replied, 'I have a friend in America who has two dachshunds. She has named one "Christopher" and the other "Lloyd".'

Christopher loved dachshund dogs and made the reputation of his own beloved Tulip through fond references to him in his writings. 'I am very honoured,' he replied.

'So you should be,' she retorted, 'they are both bitches.'

I heard the story in similar terms from both of them. It was the beginning of their much-appreciated friendship.

Christopher was impatient with garden-owners who presented themselves as great gardeners even though they were busy with another main occupation and employed gardeners to do the work. In several pointed newspaper articles, he would describe his visit to a well-known owner's garden but mention the owner only in passing, if at all. Instead he would describe in detail the working gardener who was really in charge. He then took his readers round the garden in the gardener's company, as if the owner had nothing to do with it. Sometimes, he underestimated the owners' commitment and how much they had contributed in spite of the pressures of other work. Once he described in dry detail a visit to the excellent garden of a former managing director of Pearson, the owners of the *Financial Times*, during which his host drew aside to clip a dead-head off a pink 'Frau Dagmar' rose and put it into an accompanying basket. 'I admired the pretence,' Christopher wrote, unjustly. His comment was still remembered with irritation ten years later.

Underneath these barbs lay the fact that he was a gardener who believed in gardening, at a time when gardens were fashionable but when practical, detailed work in them was in retreat. In keeping with this belief, he liked opinionated writing if he felt that it was based on observation and so I was pleased to receive an encouraging letter from him only two months after beginning to write in the *Financial Times*. I was a young nothing and he was already the experienced master but he was taken with my heartfelt assault on the nation's fondness for heather, a plant I detested in gardens. Both of us, he kindly added, owed our jobs as journalists to the support of Arthur Hellyer, then the maestro of practical journalism who wrote both for the *FT* and *Country Life*, where he had helped to appoint Christopher as a columnist. Time passed, however, and tetchiness took over. There was even a phase when whatever I wrote in the *FT* was challenged at length by Christopher in the next issue of *Country Life*. I continue to dislike the prickly purple-leaved form of berberis, but I bless it for one unattested virtue. I had written that it was a dreary plant, best suited to the gardens of a provincial hotel, whereupon Christopher wrote at length in defence of hotel gardens and purple leaves and against people who put other gardeners off. I had just bought a house with an over-developed berberis of the purple kind, so I dug it up and sent it to him by Parcel Post, telling him that I hoped he would appreciate the prickles. I had a letter back saying that he would now apply for en suite bathrooms and turn Great Dixter into a hotel.

The skirmish, which only he sustained, then fastened at random on my approval of a low-growing carpeting plant called *Phuopsis stylosa*. Christopher protested in his *Country Life* article for the following week that I had never even mentioned that it smelt of foxes but that he was not surprised as I was only a university lecturer at Oxford and had no idea what a fox smelt like. It was a badly aimed shot because my life has been divided between gardening and foxhunting and I have scented many more of the furry adversaries than Christopher had even seen in a picture book. A truce was called and ten years later I accepted his generous invitation to Dixter.

In late August, I coincided there with the last hours on earth of his famous dachshund Tulip, who was wrapped in a blanket and looking doleful, like his master. Even so, it was not all a time of melancholy. In later age, Christopher flourished on duets with his own working gardeners, one of whom, Romke, marked a new theme in Christopher's writing. He began to feature in Christopher's articles as a foil for Christopher's own sparring. When Romke left, there was a bleak winter and a slight downturn as the ageing Christopher had to cope with a garden on heavy clay and a vacancy at its head. In 1988, the gap was wonderfully filled by the young Fergus Garrett. Christopher told me he had first noticed Fergus while showing a party of students round his mixed border. He had made a characteristically teasing remark about the colour of Fergus's hair. Fergus gave a smart reply and, on seeing his talent, Christopher ended by bringing him to work at Dixter. It was an inspired combination, which also spilled over into the weekly articles, where Fergus acquired an ever-stronger presence. He transformed his patron's remaining years.

No sooner had I arrived at Dixter than I was taken out to visit the garden with the likelihood of a testing question while we walked round. Christopher had grown up when good taste in colour in gardens was being set by a country-house class who dismissed many shades as fit only for the lower orders. He had a principled objection to such narrowness and linked it to his intelligent war on convention. The colours in Dixter's longest border could be challenging, one reason why his first book, *The Mixed Border*, published in 1957, took some years to make a mark.

As we walked around, I held up my end, but marvelled at the exact, short answers which he gave to almost any question which occurred to him or me. He had the eye of a practised naturalist, alert to capsid bugs on the young shoots of a fatsia, and no less to the reasons why some, but not all, shrubby hebes have a hardy strain in their breeding. Dixter's old orchard was an early example of natural, 'meadow' gardening long before 'wildflower gardening' was pushed at us as a fashion. Christopher's supreme virtue was his exploration of the line between garden plants and plants regarded as 'wild' or only fit for nature. His range of knowledge here was encyclopaedic. He was able to look at neglected plants like woodruff or the lovely low-growing paris with sharp discrimination. He insisted, as I do, that all gardening, even wild gardening, is basically a pretence. We simulate 'Nature', our own human concept. We do not obey it.

In summer at Dixter mornings started early, with a pre-breakfast survey of the garden before 7 a.m. On my visit we stopped beneath a magnificent clematis, *flammula* I think, and Christopher told me with typical mischief that Graham Thomas had dismissed it as a second-rate variety. It looked stunning, and from the surrounding greenery Fergus emerged, weeding skilfully. We talked amiably but, as we turned to go, Christopher remarked that the tips of the left-hand edge of this enormous wall-plant were showing the first signs of wilt and should be sprayed in the next few hours. I had never even noticed them. He exemplified the view that you get as much out of gardening as you put into it. As a boy he had asked the great Miss Jekyll why her clumps of the lovely blue poppy were so big. 'Because I water them twice a day,' she replied. Bits of these poppies lived on for years in his own beds at Dixter.

Lunch, as usual, was cooked on an unmodernized stove with an obsolete buff finish. Christopher grew to love cooking, often with ingredients from the garden, but as Tulip approached death under his dog blanket, his owner drew aside and consoled himself by telling me why women are 'never any good' as garden designers. They cannot see the middle distance, he claimed. The result is a muddle of flowers without form in the foreground. I do not think that his dog's plight was clouding his sincerity.

People had a way of playing into Christopher's hands. I cherish the article in which he corrected Miss Jekyll at her most famous. She would describe how, every year, she would go out into her wood and say thanks to God because 'June is here, lovely June'. Christopher justly observed that June is a poor month in woodland as it is full of flies. The late spring shrubs are over and she really ought to have gone there in May. Women, however, could take their revenge. I once went with an enthusiastic American lady to Dixter who found Christopher by the cold frame and greeted him effusively, 'Mr Lloyd, when I last came I bought the most marvellous tin of beeswax polish for my banisters from your lovely lady wife: may I meet her and buy another?' 'She's not here,' Christopher replied with glee. Her very existence was out of the question. That same summer, I had heard how in his late seventies Christopher had been in an elevated botanical group which was assessing some of the garden beds at Kew. A young gardener with his shirt off was digging nearby, and Christopher peeled away from the group and kissed him wholeheartedly. He returned to the botanists as if nothing had happened, and made the most penetrating observation on the classification of ornamental grasses. Shortly after, the tails on his big topiary peacock birds at Dixter were docked by an intruder. Many of us enjoyed speculating who had done it and why.

Christopher loved the *FT*, especially when the music and opera critics were prominent. During one recasting of the Saturday paper, I investigated whether he would like to write on the same page, side by side with myself. The purple berberis had ceased to prickle. He said he would be delighted, but the then page editor had never heard of him and decided that a writer over seventy would be past his best. He even wrote bluntly and told Christopher as much. Christopher then refuted him by writing better than ever in *Country Life* for the next fifteen years. I regret it, because I would have been teased, corrected and greatly improved each week. He would have learned to keep off the subject of foxes.

Jardin Majorelle

Like the sale of Great Dixter and its owner's gardening accessories, the sale in Paris of the designer Yves Saint Laurent's effects in February 2009 did not pass quietly into history. The prices soared above anything so mundane as a global economic crisis. The Chinese then disputed the legal title to objects which once stood in the royal palace in old Beijing. Myself, I remembered an item which never came under the hammer: the garden in Morocco.

The Villa Oasis in Marrakech was acquired by Saint Laurent and his partner Pierre Bergé in 1981. It stood in what was the quarter then known as Serenity and came with seven acres of grounds. In 2008 Saint Laurent died after more than a decade spent largely in the villa's calm. By 2006 Bergé was estimating that the small part of the garden which is open to the public had attracted 660,000 visitors in a year. It has become one of the most visited gardens in the world.

When I saw it five years before Yves Saint Laurent's death I was almost alone among rare cactuses and bamboos, figs, cycads, and flowerpots painted in a famous shade of blue. The paths were discreetly designed beside canals and pools of water and the latticed garden pavilion to which they led had a certain charm. In the burning heat of Morocco it seemed delightful that someone so famous had made a garden with such intelligently chosen plants. I had never worn anything in the least Saint Laurent but my opinion of his taste rose with my awareness of his garden.

When I visited I had no idea that the garden is not all about Yves. It belongs in a distinctive phase of his life but it also belongs in the story of a previous French expatriate, the artist Jacques Majorelle.

Remarkably, it connects with each of their boyhoods, a time which is so often a source of the best-loved gardens. Majorelle used his boyhood to escape from his dominant father, whereas Saint Laurent never fully escaped his admiring mother. The Morocco garden connects, too, with the years of sadness and despondency which each of them lived through and confronted in its grounds.

Bergé once said that Saint Laurent, his long-term lover, was 'a man of exceptional intelligence practising the trade of an imbecile'. If so, the imbecility is remarkably interesting. Much of what I know about it derives from the excellent biography by Alice Rawsthorn, former *Financial Times* correspondent in Paris. In 1996 she published the story both of Saint Laurent's life and of his financial involvement with Bergé, his devoted promoter. I like the timeline with which she concludes. It is not a gardener's usual reading but it enables me to state that the Marrakech garden was acquired thirteen years after Saint Laurent's safari look and his designer duffel-coats in honour of Paris's student rioters (1968), ten years after he posed naked except for his spectacles (1971) and six years after the failure of his 'genderless scent' Eau Libre (1975). He bought the villa when *Le Smoking*, the male dinner-jacket, was a central theme in his female collections. In that year (1981) Yohji Yamamoto was showing prêt-à-porter in Paris for the first time and Bergé voted for Giscard d'Estaing before swiftly changing sides. In 1989 Saint Laurent's company went public on the Bourse and in the mid 1990s Bergé was fined for insider dealing.

Rawsthorn's subject was not gardening and only recently can we follow in print the clues to this garden's early life. In 2007 a philosophy teacher in Toulouse, Alain Leygonie, published an excellent book-length study of the garden and its first maker, Jacques Majorelle, who died in his mid seventies in 1962. To write it, he interviewed the surviving family and the admirable head gardener, Abderrazak Benchaâbane. I remember discovering from the villa's working gardeners that they were part of a core team of at least eight. The small enclosed area on display nowadays is very well tended but I am unable to name many of the cactuses on view, as some of them flower only every thirty years and there are no labels.

Majorelle was born in Nancy in 1886 to an artistic father whose sizeable house and garden lived on as vivid memories in his mind. He emigrated to Morocco in 1919 and four years later began to buy the ground which now includes the garden. It took another three purchases of land during nine years to round off his house and home. The style of the place was initially his vision, a combination of well-understood Moroccan vernacular style, modern architectural fashion, and traditional details and façades. Majorelle was a bold traveller in the Atlas mountains and an early admirer of the style of its village houses, from which he copied the strong 'Berber blue', now on his garden's pots and walls. It was a bold colour to import into red and ochre Marrakech. In 1931 he extended his paintings to another subject, what he called his naked negresses. The girls used to swing their hips and breasts and pose for him in what is now the Villa Oasis garden.

When the novelist Anthony Burgess interviewed Yves Saint Laurent in the 1970s, he asked him what he thought of women. He took the answer to be 'dolls', at least until Saint Laurent apologized for his franglais and explained that he had actually said 'idols'. Saint Laurent liked women and never imposed on them the homoerotic lines of clothes and body which rival designers favoured. He even used to say that women are only truly attractive as they age and their character shows in their faces. One of his models, however, remembers him pointing to her breasts and asking disapprovingly: 'What are those?' I do not think he would have wanted Majorelle's naked negresses to be reinstated in his garden.

Majorelle had a fine eye for local plants which would grow in a Moroccan garden. He also admired the colours painted on Moroccan houses. Majorelle Blue is still a recognized colour in modern paintboxes and the famous blue of the garden began in Majorelle's time. At its peak he employed twenty gardeners but between his death in 1962 and 1981 the garden went into a serious decline. Saint Laurent and Bergé then bought the house when a French company was about to develop it into a hotel and pool. With the help of two designer friends, Bill Willis and Jacques Grange, they decorated it meticulously, taking nine months to mix the right shade of red paint. Saint Laurent insisted: 'The last thing I want is a palace. I am against ultra-splendour.'

He bought chairs for $5 each and local carpets which dated from the 1930s. He was guided by the wish to realize Majorelle's dreams for the garden as they were known to him through Majorelle's widow and servants.

For Majorelle the garden was the scene of a hard divorce, then a new love in his sixties for Maithé Hammann, half-Haitian and half-German, whom he finally married. Sadly, money worries beset him, compounded by a car accident when not insured on a Moroccan mountain road which led to his loss of a leg. Yves Saint Laurent began his tenure more happily. As he had been brought up in Algeria, Marrakech took him back to childhood memories which he enhanced with the seductions of drugs and sex. His first house in Marrakech in the 1960s was known as the Villa of the Snake, where the wild parties included the young Gettys and the rock star Mick Jagger. He moved on to the Villa of Happiness, just beside Majorelle's garden, but by then his life owed more to despondency, drink and drugs. It was Bergé who renamed Majorelle's house the Villa Oasis after a favourite novel by Eugène Dabit. In the Oasis, however, Saint Laurent lived in saddened seclusion. He was most at ease there with his succession of French bulldogs.

Whereas Majorelle had had an impetuous temper, Saint Laurent struck many of his friends as childlike, before he seemed to enter old age suddenly while still only in his forties. Both of these artists deserve to be remembered for the garden in which, successively, they sought solace. When the actress Lauren Bacall appeared at a Manhattan opening wearing a smart black trouser suit, she snubbed the inquiring columnists by telling them 'if it's pants, it's Yves'. Visitors to the Villa Oasis need to understand more clearly how 'if it's plants, it's Yves' but it is also Jacques who planned the garden before him.

'Oh dear, I do love gardens!'

As the Saint Laurent garden exemplifies, flowers and gardens do not spring from our heads without a history. There are memories in us all: memories of flowers seen long ago or ideal gardens from a childhood which we can never revisit. I wrestle with my own dreams, knowing that the underlying images will never be fully realized in hard daylight.

These memories of flowers and gardens stay with us to the end. In the face of approaching death they surface with a new intensity when bunches of flowers from visitors activate these old and immovably deep memories. Quite often, the onlookers, too, turn to flowers for consolation. Édouard Manet found inspiration in vases of flowers as his life reached its end and the flower paintings of his final months are the supreme tribute to the comfort of flowers near death. Like painting, literature has its list of flower-lovers in their last days to which distinguished names continue to be added. One of them is the novelist Katherine Mansfield. She lived for four years with a diagnosis of probable death before she succumbed to tuberculosis in January 1923. Nowadays she is most widely remembered for her *In a German Pension*, a work of her youth which she later refused to have reprinted. As she realized, it does not do her justice: she should be valued as a writer who never lost her penetrating eye and critical standards. She also never lost her deep-rooted love of flowers and gardens. They are entwined fascinatingly in her published letters.

In summer 1919, she was living in her new home, 2 Portland Villas in Hampstead, turbulently married and suddenly aware of the true nature of her illness. Her friend Lady Ottoline Morrell was sending her baskets of flowers throughout the seasons from her garden in Oxfordshire, 'exquisite tulips and some sprigs of rosemary and verbena', 'peonies and delphiniums and lilac (I half expected to find the infant Moses under the irises)' and above all, the roses of which 'I am saving the petals to dry'. In mid-June, 'the sound of the wind is very loud in this house . . . Now it is dark and one feels so pale – even one's hands feel pale . . . I feel one might say anything – do anything – wreck one's own life – wreck another's.' In a note at this time she certainly spoke out: 'the red geraniums have bought the garden over my head,' she wrote. 'They are there, established, back in the old home' and 'quite determined that no power on earth will ever move them again': was she looking up at them from the lower ground floor? 'But why should they make me feel a stranger? Why should they ask me every time I go near: "And what are *you* doing in a London garden?" They burn with arrogance and pride. And I am the little Colonial walking in the London garden patch – allowed to look, perhaps, but not to linger.' Katherine Mansfield had been born in New Zealand: if she lay on the grass, she continued, the geraniums 'positively shout at me, "Look at her, lying on *our* grass, pretending she lives here . . . She is a stranger and an alien. She is nothing but a little girl sitting on the Tinakori hills and dreaming: 'I went to London and married an Englishman . . .'"'

Later in 1919 she left England for the Continent, fearful for her health, 'in the condition of a transplanted tree', as she quoted from Chekhov, 'which is hesitating whether to take root or begin to wither'. We can now follow some of her impressions through the magnificent edition of her letters. In earlier volumes there are some flowery moments as she thoughtfully emerged from the years of the Great War. She confronted that war's pervasive effects and complained, acutely, that they were not addressed by her contemporary Virginia Woolf in her novel *Night and Day*, published in 1919. In autumn of that year, flowers came to the fore in her own thinking. The life-sentence of tuberculosis had just been passed on her and in the hope of a remission she went to Italy and southern France where welcomed the fields of anemones and the local narcissi. She was delightfully happy watching the men who came to help in the garden. In north Italy, 'a big kind grey old dog in a cap' came to speak bad French to her about violets 'savage and mild' and roses that flowered in 'le mois de Noel' and a lily as big as a villa. In January she enjoyed the scent of double-flowered stocks. She walked in a floral heaven near Menton at a time when its coast was still teeming with wild flowers. It is fascinating that this young genius of a writer, exiled by her health, was lodged near Menton in months when the great Lawrence Johnston, creator of the garden at Hidcote Manor in Gloucestershire, was attending his mother in a rest-home nearby. They never met.

Katherine's excellent letters from these years are explicit about the roots of her love of flowers. They went back deep into her childhood in faraway New Zealand where her cousin Elizabeth also grew up, later Elizabeth von Arnim, made famous by her marriage to her German garden. 'When I was about the height of a garden spade,' Katherine writes in March from Menton, 'I spent weeks – months – watching a man do all these things and wandering through canes of yellow butter beans and smelling the spotted speckled broad bean flowers and helping to plant Giant Edwards and White Elephants. Oh dear, I do love gardens! I had better stop.' Constantly, her letters show her responding to cut flowers and the floral baskets which were sent to encourage her. Even under the threat of death she was dreaming of the outlines of a future garden. In January she was thinking of 'little curly blue hyacinths and white violets and the bird cherry. My trouble is that I had so many flowers when I was little. I got to know them so well that they are simply the breath of life to me. It is no ordinary love. It is a passion.'

By October 1922 medical treatments had failed and Katherine arranged to be accepted into the Institute of the legendary guru George Gurdjieff, whom her letters' editors succinctly present as 'a widely travelled Armenian Greek'. This prince of baloney had the most imposing presence and his theories of cosmic rays and curative dancing only helped to enhance his mystique. It was in Russia that he first established his Institute for the Harmonious Development of Man. After the Russian Revolution he transferred his blend of communal living, 'healing' labour and Far Eastern carpets to the Priory at Fontainebleau with the help of his newly found French supporters. Katherine Mansfield learned of him through a lecture in Paris by his accompanying

fantasist, P. D. Ouspensky. In later years the famous landscape gardener Russell Page also knew Ouspensky, just as he knew Gurdjieff,
whose natural daughter he married when she was already pregnant.
The Fontainebleau Institute and its bogus theories of 'harmony' under-
pinned Russell Page's abstract ideas about the natural world.

There is a special poignancy to Katherine Mansfield's final letters
from this farmhouse of Russian exiles and souls in need of help.
'According to Mr Gurdjieff,' she writes, 'we all of us have our "illness"
and it takes very severe measures to put us right.' For Katherine he
prescribed a hideaway above the cows in the farm barn where she
could sit 'and inhale their breath'. She duly sat up there on a pile of
carpets. Life was appallingly cold and, away from the cows, the main
business seems to have been cooking, cleaning and simply staying
alive. Hearty Russian dancing punctuated a life spent peeling carrots.
Her letters' editors propose that the company and social grouping
were what most appealed to her, and as authors live isolated lives, I can
well believe it: 'they are all very different but they are the people I have
wanted to find – real people – not people I make up or invent.' They
were so real that before long, they had stolen all her underclothes.

What did 'cosmic harmony' do for her love of flowers? Wonderfully, that love was still with her despite the hours in the cowsheds and
the intense cold and damp. The autumn of her entry to the Institute
had been a 'marvellous' year for dahlias: 'big spiked red ones, white
ones and a little bright orange kind – most lovely'. As she left Paris,
she was still recalling in letters the 'Michaelmas daisies on a solitary
bush in Acacia Road. I like them. They have such very delicate petals.'
In the Institute for Harmonious Development, in early January 1923,
she was 'looking for signs of spring already'. 'Under the espalier pear
trees there are wonderful Xmas roses ... and somebody found four
primroses the other day.' Within a day or two she was dead. She was
thirty-four years old.

The deeply felt memory of flowers had sustained her for so much
of her shortened life. Three years earlier, in Menton, she had written
home about her 'fifteen cinerarias in Italy' and how 'they grew against
the sea'. 'I hope,' she added, 'one will be able to call these things up on
one's deathbed.' I strongly believe that she could and did.

Snowdropping

Back in the English countryside, the February fashion nowadays is snowdropping. Hundreds of suitably wheeled vehicles descend on selected snowdrop collections. The dress is traditional: tweeds, waterproof jacket and a walking stick if you are still young enough to need one, not two. Snowdroppers are persons of mature experience and a battle-scarred financial history which stretches back to the 1970s. The scars are not strong enough to stop them handing over £20 for a single snowdrop which catches their fancy. I have been snowdropping with the best of them and the results have caused a slight adjustment to my views. I used to picture snowdrops on the edge of woodland or in leafy soil of a good depth where they are partially shaded and sheltered. Instinctively I would not plant them in open flowerbeds or on dry stony soil.

Visits in two directions changed my practice. The first was a visit to the poetic collection of snowdrops which was carefully accumulated near Oxford by the poet and author James Fenton during the 1990s. In his garden snowdrops were not tucked away in shade. They were started in twos or threes in raised beds, borders and cultivated ground at the base of a wall. In these places his snowdrops grew into serious clumps and allowed themselves to be divided and scattered under old-fashioned roses and between specialized alpines. The great botanical authority William Stearn considered that snowdrops hate farmyard manure and will die if they are covered in it. If Stearn had been wholly right, there would have been no future for Fenton's initial plantings of snowdrops under roses which were manured and top-dressed. In fact, snowdrops will survive mulching and manuring in moderation, although they increase even more rapidly when the manuring ceases and has been absorbed into the soil. In an Oxford Professor of Poetry's keeping, highly priced snowdrops multiplied among manure and became a portfolio of carefully chosen growth stocks. Perhaps they prefer the Muses to the rotted manure, but I had not expected to watch such distinguished selections as *plicatus* 'Colossus' or 'John Gray' increasing and allowing division after only a few years in the ground. It was unexpected to find a summer border under-planted with the excellent *nivalis* 'Anglesey Abbey' and to see old roses carpeted with a tall, early charmer called 'Limetree'. This variety's academic credentials are impeccable. It is said to have been discovered under the very lime tree beneath which the keen mind of R. A. Butler used to relax while writing his Education Act, the framework for Britain's post-war teaching.

The lesson from Fenton's garden of the Muses is that a collection of snowdrops will develop steadily in ground which has been well manured, away from shade or grass, and will enliven bare flowerbeds in a changeable February. Individual bulbs of named varieties are expensive, but they are not feeble and as many of them spread quickly, they soon seem a reasonable buy. I noted down the large-flowered 'Mighty Atom' and the early 'Castlegar' from Ireland which starts to flower just before Christmas, a wondrous sight. There is a particular charm in 'Neill Fraser', a single Scottish variety with rounded flowers which were greatly admired by the connoisseur E. A. Bowles. With Fenton it flourished in a flowerbed in open sunlight. For vigour, 'Galatea' and 'Magnet' are unsurpassed, even under a well-manured rose hedge.

My second instructive visit was to the supreme collection of snowdrops maintained at Colesbourne Park, Gloucestershire, off the A435 between Cirencester and Cheltenham. The collection goes back to the great tree planter and gardener H. J. Elwes, whose great-grandson still lives in the house, and in February it attracts hundreds of snowdroppers willing to follow its signposted trail. The surrounding arboretum and water are a fine sight, especially from vantage points carpeted with yellow aconites. A sharp eye for a tree has continued to run in the Elwes family and a visit to Colesbourne is pleasant enough even if you look upwards into the trees' branches rather than downwards at *Galanthus elwesii* around your feet.

The initial part of the visitors' walk runs under tall trees beside carpets of Britain's native snowdrop, *Galanthus nivalis*. A spectacular mass of the vigorous snowdrop 'S. Arnott' is one of the sights of this part of the garden and shows what a superb choice this old Scottish variety is on almost any soil. The provost of Dumfries sent bulbs of it down to H. J. Elwes in this very garden. It is fine to see their descendants flowering by the hundred in this same home and giving off a sweet scent in the sunshine, to those who kneel down and check it out.

The second part of the trail leads round the house into less expected territory. In sunny beds beneath walls or among border plants, fine snowdrops are also flowering freely and forming divisible clumps. I do not think that poetry runs in the Elwes family, but many of the most expensive snowdrops are happy here too with a life in the open rather than under the canopy of tall trees. The soil at Colesbourne is no better than mine and refutes the view that special snowdrops insist on special leafy conditions. Mrs Elwes told me how some of the best clumps in the woodland grow on Cotswold brash without any depth of soil beneath. As proof she pointed to her special discovery, the old snowdrop 'George Elwes', which is named after her son. She found it among tree roots and had to dig destructively in order to acquire large bulbs for transplanting and eventual re-sale.

Among such diversity it is hard to name the flowers accurately, let alone to tell a double 'Cordelia' from a double 'Hippolyta'. My success rate at naming was only four varieties out of every ten, and even then, I sometimes saw a label. The experts, too, have their disagreements. I had started the day by admiring superb clumps of the wild Greek *Galanthus gracilis*, whose leaves are distinctively narrow and twisted. At Colesbourne, however, some of the clumps called *gracilis* show no twisting at all. Fortunately, we have an authoritative botanical guide, Aaron P. Davis's *The Genus Galanthus*, a magnificent work of reference published by Kew Gardens and the Timber Press, but even Davis has his moments of uncertainty. Snowdrops have intermarried, bred and multiplied, often from ancestors which have been left in peace in country gardens since the nineteenth century. Near the end of his life, the great gardener Lewis Palmer found other people's names and identities confusing and used to complain that if only they were as distinct as snowdrops they would be easy to sort out. The rest of us will never pin all snowdrops to a family tree.

Nor can we pin them down to rigid rules. The standard practice nowadays is to dig up their clumps when still in leaf and split them for immediate replanting. Even the experts differ over the best timing, some recommending action just before the snowdrops are in full flower, some preferring to wait until the flowers have gone. In my experience, bulbs which are transplanted before the flowers open are even more likely to flower well in the following spring. My light soil is tolerated by snowdrops, but is not ideal for them. At Colesbourne, the garden director follows a third option: he plants snowdrop bulbs in autumn when no leaves show. So long as the bulbs have not dried out, they will move very well in autumn too. Drying out is their problem in the mass-market trade, but not in private gardens. At Colesbourne, thousands of clumps prove that autumn transplanting still works.

Gardening in Texan Adversity

Like snowdrops, many gardens have to grow in hard conditions. Nonetheless, gardening in adversity always encourages me, and when seen abroad it stops our complaints about local problems. What is a hot summer in England to gardeners who have had to cope with years of drought in Australia? What is a badger or two to gardeners in America who are invaded by urban deer? In February I widened my grasp of adverse gardening by research in that land of plenty, Texas.

One plant from this home of oil rigs and wildcat drillers is familiar to British readers: the Texas yellow rose. During the wars with Mexico in the 1830s, the Texan generals profited from a secret weapon who was active behind the Mexican lines. She was Emily, a young lady of mixed-race origin, a 'yellow' in Texan language of the time. Taken captive, she was assigned one of the least challenging missions in military history: to seduce a senior Mexican after lunch. She duly bagged the top general and sent a message to the Texans, who promptly attacked his leaderless troops. In her memory the yellow rose became a Texan icon. At home I grow *Rosa × harisonii* 'Harison's Yellow', the rose which that supreme gardener from the American south, Nancy Lancaster, always told me was the right Texan yellow. It flowers in late May on a prickly bush about three feet high and will grow anywhere.

Out in Houston the temperatures in early spring rival those of an English June and are hot enough to bring the Texan yellow rose into early flower. When I ventured out on to a highway running westwards from the city I felt less envious. In summer the Texan heat is debilitating and if rain ever comes, it falls in a brief deluge. When summer breaks, tempests are then a threat in the wake of tornadoes. In Houston itself, the soil is usually a heavy black clay which is unworkable when it dries out. The sunny spring skies are lovely, but the temperatures can drop to several degrees of sharp frost at night, enough to ruin many plants which would best survive the hot summer. Keen gardeners warned me of the worst hazard: freak bouts of very cold weather which blows down from the far north in a wind corridor. It is known as the Alberta Shuttle and was at its worst in 1983.

In late February, therefore, I did not expect too much when I called on a great rarity, a Texan garden supported by its own Foundation on ten acres of tough soil beside a busy road an hour's journey west of Houston. Further along the road middle-aged motorbikers meet for hamburgers at the Thirsty Parrot Café. Wild pigs live in the surrounding woodland and crawfish burrow up among the garden's plants wherever the soil is soft. I had not reckoned with the founder and owner of Peckerwood Garden, the softly spoken John Fairey, who is now in his late seventies. He started to garden on this patch of adversity in 1971, but has made it into a Texan treasure by a thoughtful reaction to its natural limitations. He has given it years of hard work and has applied the eye for beauty which has sustained his career as a teacher of design. His aim is to teach students how to see differently and in his garden he offers the lesson to us all. He is one of those calm optimists whose skills as a gardener I recognize from long experience. If I was a plant, I would grow for him.

Peckerwood Garden is a lesson in how to work with adversity. John Fairey has not spent a fortune in trying to change local conditions. In 1988, he began making expeditions into Mexico's mountains across the border in order to collect seed from hardy but drought-resistant flora which would survive in the difficult Texan conditions. By experiment, he learned the best ways of germinating these unusual plants, and before long he was supplying Kew Gardens and other botanical institutes with his collections. He was joined on his trips by various British plant-collectors, James Compton and Martyn Rix among them, many of whose foreign collections are important for gardeners too. Enhanced from Mexico, Peckerwood Garden is informally planned as a shrub and tree garden with a changing layer of bulbs and low planting. It contains more than 3,000 species, ranging from unfamiliar Japanese oaks to excellent magnolias and scented mahonias. It is a garden for close inspection by plant-lovers, although they will struggle to name many of the best sights of the moment.

I first realized that Fairey was special when we passed a climbing plant on a flimsy fence in his front gravel garden. I did not recognize it, but he told me it was a climbing philadelphus, or scented mock orange. I know this family well in British catalogues but I never knew that some members of it are natural climbers. We went on past unfamiliar Mexican yuccas and grey-green agaves, including a sharp-toothed one which Fairey has named Jaws. My notebook was already working overtime and we had not even reached the small-flowered camellias from Japan. I became truly lost among the mahonias. Admittedly, we had just seen the first single white flowers on a rare bloodroot under some fine shrubs, but I was not expecting to see the Mexican *Mahonia pallida* which has delicate heads of pale lemon-yellow flowers. Word had been reaching me of new, delicate members of this family, but I never expected to be enchanted by them within earshot of a highway in Texas. These Mexican forms of mahonia are hardy and are sure to become a mainstay of gardens as stocks in British nurseries build up.

I could make no more sense of Peckerwood's hardy magnolias, especially the evergreen forms from Mexico. The garden's superb oaks were no more familiar, least of all the hardy evergreen oaks from Japan. Even our own nursery experts, including Hillier's, have been importing seed from Peckerwood of these new collected forms. In a British garden I would be happy to look up through the branches of Peckerwood's ten-year-old *Quercus glauca*, the Japanese blue oak. The hardiest such oak is the most beautiful, *Quercus myrsinifolia*, the bamboo-leaf oak, with long, narrow leaves which are a shining green on top and slightly grey underneath.

Thankfully, I recognized some of the garden's white-flowering halesia trees and began to understand how the mature areas had been planted with an artist's eye for the trunks and bark of the tallest trees. They are set off by a recurring use of the softer grey tones in Mexican yuccas and rare hardy forms of palm. America has justly famous botanical gardens and arboretums but the most impressive private gardens tend to be backed by their owners' personal fortunes and to pay respect to established European or Japanese styles. Peckerwood is different, the work of a single owner during nearly forty years of his thoughtful collecting and planting. It has grown to need supporting staff and now needs to be assured of a long, public life by a benefactor with the intelligence to work with its creator in the later years of his life and guide the garden for the future.

John Fairey kept on impressing me by his resilience. Sure, a tornado took out some of his trees in 1983 but as a result new ones could be tried in their place. Sure, the crocuses die out after a year and the tulips fare no better, but you can then grow carpets of ipheion in their place. If the climate is difficult, think out of the box and go out and collect seed in an under-explored zone with similar natural problems. Even the local wild pigs are a fact of life, to be countered with a special sort of hog-trap, baited with corn. After taking notes in Texas, I will think twice about going into a decline at the first patter of a squirrel's feet. In Texas there are urban gardeners who wrap their early flowering camellias in fairy lights and illuminate them on chilly spring evenings. Perhaps I should wrap up my badgers in last year's lights off the Christmas tree and watch them make colour patterns as they excavate the lawns.

Weevils in Charge

Whether in Texas or chilly northern Tyneside, burn your old copies of *Spare Rib;* pulp *The Female Eunuch*; melt down your sorority pins. For more than thirty years, feminists have been declaring Gender War, but it looks out of date when seen from the level of the soil. No feminist author has ever realized it, but while they have been telling women to burn their bras and take over the show, a population within feet of their armchairs has long done exactly that. Even the great Aristophanes would have to run for cover. It is not just a case of females running the state. Close to us all, females have been managing for centuries without any sign of a male at all.

In a research greenhouse near Dusseldorf, I became aware of this neglected dimension to issues of sexual politics. In order to understand the fellow inhabitants of our planet, we need to talk to the people whose living depends on combating the pests in its population. Under the glass roofs of Germany's chemical Bayer Group, I inspected a sickly pelargonium in a flowerpot and learned that it was the consequence of Females In Charge. It was a barely living answer to the question with which every couple have tormented themselves: would things go better if women took over? Within walking distance of Germaine Greer, a female population has been teeming in pot plants, compost and many of the plantings which she buys in containers from garden shops.

For years, I have dreaded the very name of Vine Weevil, believing that it is one of the few menaces which have not yet invaded my garden. It attacks roots, slaughters fuchsias and punches the margins of healthy leaves. The expert Helen Dillon tells us to check our bergenias if we want to know if we have vine weevils. If the edge of a bergenia leaf has been clipped as if by a ticket collector, then vine weevils are in the garden. Holes in the middle of the leaf are due to slugs, not weevils. So far, I only have slugs.

After visiting Dusseldorf, I am even more thankful that vine weevils have not yet discovered me. The truth may be familiar to entomologists, but is ignored by social theorists and harassed gardeners: the population of the vine weevil is exclusively female. Nobody is sure what happened to the last of the males. On one view he did not survive the Ice Age. In my view, the females bit him to death in the locker room. They had discovered how to cope very well without him because they had learned a hideous truth: how to reproduce without sex.

The implications are extremely suggestive. Theologically, I do not think that the vine weevil has yet been taken into account. For tens of thousands of years the females have been reproducing prolifically by virgin birth. They are thought to produce up to 1,200 eggs in a month and their children hatch into a single-sex family which keeps the weevil sisterhood strictly to its orientation. In the 1970s we briefly lost control of this all-female world. Until then, male gardeners had dealt with it in a masculine way. They had sprayed it to death with DDT and stopped females getting the upper hand. When DDT was banned, females started to proliferate. What sort of society have they decided to run?

For a start, they dispensed with the traditional barriers of colour. Manifestly, they have decided that the polarization between blacks and whites is masculine and unacceptable; their grubs are creamy white and mature to a dull shade of black. I need hardly add that the entire female adult population is thick-skinned and completely unsquashable. The little lady weevils, according to expert informants, 'are said to resemble space creatures'. To show that they will be fit to join a hen night, they grow up legless. Most of their activity occurs by night, including virgin-birthing. They hate the winter with a truly feminine hatred. Not until May and June do they dust off their space-age suits and set about building a new society.

The result is parasitic and extraordinarily aggressive. They begin life as if up a pole, hiding in the leaves of plants on which they punch a ticket-collector's imprint. They then come down, burrow into the base of a plant, and disappear below ground. They are extremely hard to catch when misbehaving and their main aim is to ruin the roots of anything which grows. If they feel threatened, they hide under a central bulb or corm. This habit makes them a menace in pots full of cyclamen. Their entire attitude to life is blinkered, focused and obsessive. All they want to do is to ruin as many of the surrounding roots and plants as possible and to eat lunch and dinner without becoming fat. They are much happier indoors where it is warm than outdoors where the weather will spoil their complexions. They revel in a soft, squishy compost, especially peat. As a result, they have been multiplying alarmingly since the introduction of black polythene containers and spongy peat compost. Every weekend, when gardeners drive down to the garden centre for a pot-bound shrub, they risk bringing back with it a microcosm of a virgin female society. The shrub's compost is likely to be riddled with vine weevils, invisible to most human eyes.

Life's major question thus seems to be answered. If there were nothing but females in the world, they would start by making short work of the curtains, then savage the soft furnishings and go and hide under the sofa. Other questions are more awkward. What would they do if they saw a man and how can we exterminate these virgin creepers in our post-DDT age? The possibility of introducing a man and answering the first of these questions is tantalizing. You may remember Basil Ransom in Henry James' novel *The Bostonians*. 'The masculine character, the ability to dare and endure, to know and not to fear reality, to look the world in the face and take it for what it is ... this is what I want to preserve.' I propose that our ingenious scientists use their genome knowledge, build a male vine weevil, instil Basil Ransom's qualities and let him loose on the female population. Imagine the poor little virgins when they see him coming. Will they think of him as fit only for speculation and parasitic trading? Will they cluster, and charge him out of the compost? I like to think that deep down in their post-glacial consciousness, they will feel a mysterious, buried dimension stirring. They will go round in south-westerly circles and suddenly find that they have fallen in love. The effect on a potted poinsettia will be shattering, but we ought to send this feminist enclave the only Valentine it will appreciate.

3. *Rudbeckia hirta* 'Prairie Sun'

ncy Lancaster
th her hose at
aseley Court

Lady-Killing Progress

For thoughtful gardeners, the question remains: how can we exterminate these all-female vine weevils in an era when DDT is banned? There is no effective 'organic' answer and without chemical weaponry, gardening and farming would degenerate into chaos. Fortunately chemists have come up with a compound to kill the ladies off. It was discovered by males and is marketed as Provado in garden centres, where it is labelled 'The Ultimate Bug Killer'. I repent of my occasional complaints that gardeners are sold less effective chemicals than those available to farmers. The hard commercial fact is that without farming, gardeners would never be treated to new chemical allies in the first place. Provado is based on an active compound which was developed by chemists at Bayer in 1985 from research which began in 1972. It cost Bayer more than $100 million to develop the compound and bring it through ever more stringent tests for licensing. By itself the gardening market cannot sustain the risks and costs of developing a new product. New chemicals which we buy as gardeners have been widely available to farmers for ten years already.

The chemical breakthrough became known as Imidacloprid and worked wonders in the years before gardeners could buy it openly. The 'green movement' needs to recognize that Imidacloprid is one of the saviours of the cotton crops in Turkey, the citrus crops from the Aegean eastwards and acres of those 'farm-fresh' tomatoes which we buy because they have been grown within sight of open country. In Italy, Imidacloprid is being used to prevent the yellowing of leaves on the plane trees which line roads. Imidacloprid kills whitefly, blackfly, greenfly and the proliferating lily beetle. It destroys an all-female invasion by vine weevils and protects plants against them for at least six months. When you next buy an unwaxed lemon in a wholefood shop and congratulate yourself on your organic custom, remember that citrus crops were at risk to the citrus leaf miner in 1990 and that without Imidacloprid there would be no lemons to wax or unwax anyway.

Nonetheless, Imidacloprid is a chemical. Before 'green' gardeners protest, it degrades very quickly in sunlight. It does not wash out into the water supply because it binds itself loosely, but unshakeably, to particles in the soil. Provado Pest Free is the brand recommended for amateur gardeners. In Britain, packets carry the statutory warning 'high risk to bees', but it applies only to bees who are wrongly targeted with this compound head-on. Provado Pest Free should be used to drench the soil, not to spray straight on to bees or insects in the air. It can be sprayed on to plants in leaf, but should be kept away from plants in flower. It will then not affect pollinators and is harmless to bees unless they are sprayed with it directly in the face. Professional brands with Imidacloprid have been stringently tested and licensed for use on such fundamental crops as sugar beet, hops and lettuces. It is so safe for mammals that it is used to kill fleas on pets. It could also be used to kill nits in children's hair.

Imidacloprid does not deter insects from feeding on a plant which has been treated with it. This effect is crucial, because other chemicals simply drive bugs away to another type of plant. It is taken up by root hairs into the plant's general system and acts systemically, killing only the bugs which eat it. Its method of killing is extremely ingenious. All-female weevils and other insects have nervous systems which transmit impulses from 'releasers' to specific receptors. Most of the previous chemical killers attacked the 'releasers', but Imidacloprid blocks the receptors. As the experience is a new one, the population has no resistance. Brands of Imidacloprid are a godsend against the termites which ruin house-timbers and buildings in Japan and America. No longer is it a case of Termites On Top. I wonder how organic enthusiasts expect to protect their decking in such climates if they refuse the use of all chemicals.

I know how I protect my fragile bedding-plants. I now water the

1. The author advances thoughtfully into his Oxfordshire garden in

2 Parterre at Brécy in winter

1. The author advances thoughtfully into his Oxfordshire garden in mid-July

2 Parterre at Brécy in winter

3. *Rudbeckia hirta* 'Prairie Sun'

4. Nancy Lancaster
with her hose at
Haseley Court